AGAPE
THE
INTENT
OF THE
SOUL

EVA HERR

www.evaherr.com

I dedicate this book to my father,
Norman Flack.

AGAPE

(*pronounced ah-gah'-pay*)
is a Greek word meaning
unselfish love of one person for another.

TABLE OF CONTENTS

PART I: THE BEGINNING

PART II MICHAEL, SETH AND THOMAS

Acknowledgements

I would like to thank my husband, Howard, and my children, Zachary, Jessica and Derek, for their patience and tolerance throughout the writing of this book. I would also like to thank my friends Maxine Taylor, Sheryl Adair and Chuck for their editing help, Roy Scruggs for his advice on physics and my friends Roy Mills, Mel and Alice Minitor, Dannion Brinkley, Raymond Moody, Candace Apple, Judge Joel Feldman, Jack Hall, Jr., Kirby Turnage, Satyam Nadeen, John Zitello, Dr. Claude Swanson, Michael Holloway, John Marcum, Julie Latzko, Nigel Yorwerth, Patricia Spadaro and Robyn Andrews Quail for their invaluable and interminable support. Without them, there would be no book.

AGAPE, UNCONDITIONAL LOVE

Agape, or unconditional love, is the complete intent of the soul. It is the entire purpose of existence for all there is. Without it, one can only stumble through eternity and wonder what problem it next faces. One would have nothing to live for or yearn for. With this single item can a soul find everything needed for the survival and happiness of mankind. Without it there is nothing but a lousy existence. With it one can accomplish anything one dreams to accomplish, not just for the one, but for all. It is this unconditional love that will bring a future of happiness not only for ourselves, but our children. Without it, a world of calamity and destruction awaits our children. What is it you want for your children? A world of peace and happiness or a world of blackness and embers? The choice is yours, but the choice must be made soon, or there will be no choice.

PART I

CHAPTER 1

The Kidnapping

I was six years old when I first experienced physical abuse that I actually recall. I was in the backyard playing and my mother was angry because I hadn't washed the dishes. She came at me, fists clenched and grabbed me by the hair. I was so shocked all I knew to do was run. Running didn't help though because she could run faster. When she caught me, she whipped me so hard I literally couldn't sit without pain in my legs. This I came to learn was the pattern for life.

During this time, my evolved father, just knew he had a genius for a daughter and constantly plagued me with various types of knowledge. He thought the more information he put in front of me, the smarter I would be. Little did he know at that time I would be doing this for a living. In any event, he was a wonderful, kind man, I really think he had the "gift" too, it was just undeveloped. (I can remember him attempting to talk to me about physics, parallel dimensions experiencing all at one time and other such topics when I was younger, but I had absolutely no idea what he was talking about.) However, he was a perfectionist with obsessive-compulsive tendencies and addiction problems.

The first two alone are bad enough, but that mixed with alcohol was a dangerous combination, much like a time bomb waiting to go off. And off they will go without some sort of spiritual intervention to take place, what I call a "dark night of the soul." I endured strict discipline for anything less than perfection. So he produced a daughter with no self confidence whatsoever because nothing was ever good enough.

So, it seemed, the little girl began to outshine the mother. The mother was no longer the morning glory, in more ways than one. The little girl see, didn't grow up a morning glory, she grew into a ruby red rose. The closer to perfection the rose grew, the more strangled for light the morning glory became.

And that, is how it all began.

Now we will move from the formulative years to the pre-teen era of my life. As I grew, I believe memories of my mother's own childhood began to haunt her. The closer I became into developing as a woman, the more my mother began to see herself in me. I believe this was very frightening to her because she didn't have a very pleasant childhood. The woman, with many injustices performed upon her by adults, grew up hating the world and for valid reasons. She had no education and knew not what lie outside the boundaries of her own expectations. So what happened was expectations in my mother's life were placed upon me. What is the mirror of expectations? Unmet expectations and a revenge for the rest of the world. That is all she knew, so that is what she taught me. She taught me how to defend myself against the world by having to defend myself from her almost every day of my life. This was a constant battle as I grew. For when those injustices were performed against her, she was young and naïve. It took her innocence but with it came a closeness she had never experienced. She associated that closeness with love, so submitted. She later learned it was a mistake, but the damage was done. She forgot about a child having been seduced by an adult and carried the burden that was a bad person because she submitted.

If you tell yourself everyday of your life that you are a bad person; expect to behave as and be considered by your peers as, a bad person. Whatever you imagine that to be, you will be to all, because we are all one.

I can remember when I first began to show an interest in boys, she cut my hair off. I remember it as if it were yesterday. I had this long, dark, thick mane of hair, all the way to my waste. It was the summer between the 5th and 6th grade and this particular weekend she and two cohorts cut my hair to about and inch or two in length. I was absolutely devastated. I hid under the table the entire night. I looked just like a boy as far as I was concerned. In addition, I was a shy child and my hair was my security. It was all gone with a snip of the scissors. Smiles on their faces, tears on mine.

What resulted was a young girl scorned by her own mother. In fact, I don't believe I had realized the significance of that action until this moment. I know you are dying to know now if it makes me angry and I can honestly say it does not. It's almost as if it is all someone else's life at this point. However, what resulted from the humiliation of that public scorn was a girl who would not tolerate public humility by others ever again, if it was within her power. The girl learned to stand up for her beliefs. For it is your beliefs that determine who you are and where you are in life. Without that lesson learned how would this book be here? It would not have been written for the girl wouldn't be who she is today.

Evidently, my mother enjoyed sex, but she didn't like to have it with the same person all of the time and this proved to be a problem to my father because he was a man that took the vows of marriage seriously.

My mother though was now raising a daughter and the last thing she wanted was a sexually promiscuous daughter. So she had to teach me all those things *not* to do that she did. Though I understand this thought process now, I had no idea what was actually occurring at the time. She constantly accused me of having sexual relations when I was still a virgin. She just could not get it in her head that I was a different girl.

She had no idea of what healthy sexual relations were so she decided I would have sexual relations over her dead body. Little did she know that at the time I had absolutely no idea what she was talking about.

Now we are going to move to the 6th grade, that's when things really started getting ominous. Though I will mention that throughout the 5th grade mother's behavior was less than admirable when it came to racial equality. She, and others would stand at the bus entrance and refuse to allow the bus to enter the school property. Unbeknownst to her, I was literally sharing a seat with a black girl, Jacqueline. There were not enough chairs for us all and I offered to share my seat with her and she accepted. I never told my mother about that, but I don't know that it would have made a difference.

Anyway, back to the original story line. The girl that entered the sixth grade that year was forever damaged due to the uncivilized behavior of a mother that summer. A mother that had really loved her, she just loved her like a tool. A tool to get things she wanted for herself. The damage caused at the expense of the girl was never a concern. That year of the 6th grade started a cycle that I am happy to say, I stopped.

My mother became obsessed with my activities and whether or not I was having sex. She went through every personal item I owned on a regular basis. She covered every inch of my room from drawer bins to closets. I can tell you one thing, her behavior was not consequential for any behavior of mine. She just did it. She would find various communications with friends, but nothing inappropriate. From there she would search the boy out who showed interest in me, telling them what they better not do to her daughter. I had always wondered why I never had any dates in high school. She would then befriend the boy and hit on him right in front of my eyes. It was a site to be seen.

This, of course didn't occur until high school or thereabouts, but it was a rampant behavior of hers. It was a behavior that continued until the day she died. She used this behavior in an attempt to control my first marriage. It worked too, to a great or lesser degree. It affected it enough that we later divorced and I don't think either of us ever really knew why it happened because I certainly loved him and it was I who filed. All with mother's encouragement, of course. It was at this time she began to focus on my son.

She began to have turmoil with my brother and his wife. She knew too that her own husband, the man she left my father for, was having an affair, or two. She began to notice that there was a new baby in the world and she could shift her focus to that because a baby could love in return and fed her need for love. She was getting older now and her drive for sex was waning.

Zachary suddenly became all there was to her. Our relationship became better than it had ever been because I had something wanted. Mother began to covet that child beyond all else in life. She began to plan the demise of my marriage clearing a path that could possibly have Zachary under the same room with her. She baited us both against each other and like fools, we both fell for it, unknowingly, of course.

After the divorce, the plan was for Zachary and I to live with her. This did not work. I agreed to allow him to finish the school year, which was around the corner. The deal being I would spend time with him on weekends at my new apartment. He would stay with her during the week for school until it let for summer.

That was the biggest mistake I had ever made in my life and I didn't know it. I had opened the door for inappropriate attachment and hadn't known it. She began to take on the belief that he was hers. Mother had taken the form of cradle robber and

I had no idea. I thought it was grandmother's love. Her sickness though evident, was unknown to me at the time, for it was all I knew.

When I moved to Atlanta, that was the last straw, it was the last bit of self restraint she had. She had to have him now. I was out of her control. First I got out of her house, when that didn't work, I moved out of state. From that moment in time, though I didn't know, I became her enemy. I became the object of the wrath of a scorned woman and it was about to hit me like the wrath of hell–and I just didn't know it. She worked at massaging our relationship. I thought life was great. My mother had began to act with human civility, I had a job I loved with a good income. I was on the path to a new life. Things were great until that November when I told her I had met a man and he was Jewish.

I forgot to mention that I had a child support hearing pending in Alabama about this same time. Two or three weeks prior, my attorney had informed me that I need to pay X amount of dollars by X date in order for him to try the case. I had complained to my mother about how expensive the day-care was in Atlanta, I had not been prepared for the exorbitance. I had also shared with her my need to raise the money for trial. She never said a word. In any event, I lived in a gated apartment complex in a nice neighborhood. I made arrangements for Zachary to ride the bus home after school and let himself in. A neighbor would check on him. I had no choice, I had to raise the money and I couldn't do that and pay for day-care and late fees.

That was it. Her plan was ready to be implemented. She would wait until the perfect time and come take him. She had been to see a lawyer, she had a plan. She would intervene in my child support action by alleging I wasn't a good mother. She would rather do that than come and stay with me for a few weeks. After all, she didn't work. She would get away with this because she never "served" or notified me of her intervention in the case. Obviously, since I had no knowledge of her filing, I had no knowledge of the hearing so I did not show up. By statute, the judge had to grant the motion for her to have temporary custody.

She had done it right before my very own eyes, it was I who so stupidly trusted her with a key. I knew better. She had taken my child, my world and I grieved with hate at her betrayal. No betrayal could be worse. This was betrayal of love for lust for that which belonged to someone else, my son.

At this point, I experienced hate unlike I had ever experienced an emotion in my life. This was the beginning of my enlightenment and again, I just didn't know it.

I never dreamed a mother would do something like that to her own daughter, especially mine. Though I don't know why. She not only took someone's child, she took her own daughter's child. The woman seemed to have no boundary that she would respect.

I had been witness to many bad deeds performed by this woman, but never anything involving human life. She was messing with the universe, she was placing into motion, negative energy. It was negative thought, intent and an electrical impulse sending it out into the world. The result eventually being the loss of her own life. Love and hate issues store in the heart and don't think for one minute that I wasn't sending her thoughts of hate, because I was! The dark night of the soul was around the corner.

It was upon me. My son was gone, I lost my job, I was pregnant and my father died. All in about six weeks. No where to run, no where to hide. It was here as black as night. This man was sent by an angel to take care of me during this traumatic time in my life. He needed someone needy and submissive and I needed to stay alive. Though I have to say I loved this man. He is a special man. He has chosen to learn respect for women and self esteem issues through me and I have chosen to learn control and oppression through him.

What happened next that would somewhat traumatize me is that she would come to my house and say things that literally made me grit my teeth. She would say what a wonderful woman and mother I was but when I turned around she would whisper to my friend what a horrible mother I was. Which was it?

Then she began to go with me to watch my husband play tennis tournaments. I would cringe with embarrassment as she would say loud, negative comments about the opposing player, sometimes just inches away from his relative. See, my husband is a professional tennis player and we see these same people over and over, year after year and become friends. We socialize together and there was my mother making negative comments. I finally had to explain to her that these people were our friends and that there was an expected rule of etiquette in tennis to be quiet.

Another constant problem through the years and one that continued was that of her contacting my friends as if they were hers and say negative things. Same ole, same ole. It was time for her to be removed from my life again. She could not behave. We went through the appropriate behavior thing several times. Meaning she would be sent home and not allowed back until she admitted her actions and apologized to the appropriate parties.

From there we went to the taking of my personal possessions. She would come for a visit and I would inevitably find something missing when she left. It didn't have to be much, she just liked to take my things. I would ask her about the missing item, only to have her deny the allegation, but be insulted that I had asked. After she died, I recovered some of my things, but many were gone forever.

She is missed from my life, but I have to admit there is less chaos.

After her death, there were still more surprises. At her funeral I saw a woman approaching to console me. I knew this woman as the signatory of a very nasty affidavit about me. I backed from her asking why she would want to say such awful things about me when she had never before met me and then want to hug me? She never signed an affidavit, my mother and one of her cohorts had forged it.

I then went inside the funeral home where I saw my step brother in law, who I avoided. My mother had always told me that he and my step sister refused to come to her house if I was there during holidays–so why should I want to be consoled by him? He finally cornered me and asked why I was avoided him. The look on his face was that of obvious shock. She had done it again, but at least I knew the truth.

That first Christmas after her death, my aunt handed me a small package. When opened it revealed a ring that she had found in one of my mother's jean pockets. It was the same ring my mother had spent two hours helping me search for when it went missing. My mother had it all the time.

The disclosure of the Will was a shock as well. She left most everything to our step-father, along with a bunch of bills and funeral expenses.

My poor grandmother received the worst surprise. Her roof was leaking and she attempted to draw money from her savings to repair the roof. My mother had taken every single cent. Her life savings were all gone...and her roof still leaks.

*And the story begins...*I had no money, no place to go and absolutely no one to turn to. In one short month I had lost my job, I was pregnant again and unmarried, and, worst of all, my own mother had kidnapped my six-year-old son. The kidnapping was just one more thing I would hate my mother for, another episode in a long line of abuses and torments I thought would never end. Yet this latest torture, as painful as it seemed to me at the time, would catapult me into a new world–a world of enlightenment and spiritual insight beyond what I could ever imagine.

A few months before, I had left my hometown in Alabama

in search of a new life. I needed to get away from the memories of a terrible divorce and from my controlling and emotionally unstable mother. Knowing better, I had stayed with her after my divorce to try and recuperate. But she had not only abused me physically while I was there, but when I moved out she smashed the windows of my new apartment to get inside. Desperate to escape from this insanity, I packed everything I owned, stuffed it in my car and U-Haul and camped out with my son for three weeks in the woods of John Tanner State Park in Atlanta. I would get up early in the morning, shower in a park facility and then head out for the day, my son in tow, to hunt for a job.

I finally found a place to live and a new job as a litigation paralegal. I decided that I was going to spend time with my son, Zachary, and not even think about a new relationship. Barely had I settled into my new life when, of course, I met someone and it was love at first sight. This new someone was a wonderful Jewish man. Having grown up as a Southern Baptist, my parents–especially my mother–were none too happy. Zachary would be better off with her in Alabama, she decided, as far away from this Jewish man as possible. Since, of course, I didn't consent, my mother devised a plan. A few weeks later, just five days before Christmas, she kidnapped Zachary.

Taking away my son was not enough. She also called me constantly and wrote letters telling me that God had placed my son on earth for her. She had abandoned my brother and me when we were kids and she now claimed that Zachary was her second chance. She even called my workplace, harassing my boss and other people I worked with until they could stand it no more and let me go. She was trying to do everything she could to force me back to Alabama so she could control my life and rid me of this Jewish man.

I was desperate and needed emotional support, but I didn't know where to turn. My family—my mother's mother, my mother's sister, my father, my brother, his wife—were all afraid of my mother and wouldn't stand up to her. They stood by and watched me fall to the pits of hell, each whimpering to me that they could do nothing.

I tried to turn to my father. My parents were divorced and my father had nothing to do with my son's kidnapping. He had loved my mother, and he still loved her. But he knew he didn't have the strength to go against her internal rage brought about by emotional instability and long-standing mental illness. My mother had abused him for decades. She had abused me for decades. My father had always told me that my mother, an aging beauty, was jealous of my beauty. She wanted to live her life through mine. She envied my job, my friends and most of all, me. Being the daughter of a mother filled with envy for who you were was a tough battle to win. Eventually, she abandoned our family. She ran off with her boss, not even telling us where she was or how we could contact her. It was left up to me to raise my brother while my father worked. My poor father struggled through each day the best he could, but the grief was evident. Over time, the regret ate her alive. Astoundingly, I came to understand that she didn't regret depriving us of love; she regretted that she had been deprived of our love.

After years of enduring my mother's abuse, my father, a kind and wise man, had finally turned to alcohol to escape the pain. That was how he dealt with the taking of my son too. I begged and pleaded with him to help me, but my mother was too overpowering and the alcohol too suppressive. He had no motivation to live, much less fight a crazy woman. My mother allowed me to visit Zachary on Christmas day for a few hours and Dad was there. I was consumed with anger for his lack of action, so words were few and emotions high. I didn't know it was the last time I would ever see him alive.

CHAPTER 2

The Battle for My Son and My Life

Completely overwhelmed with grief at the taking of my son, I was worn down, depressed and lacked the energy to carry on with life. On top of everything else, I awoke one morning to find my breasts swollen and sore. I knew what that meant. I took a pregnancy test, but I already knew the results.

Triggered by my mother's abuse, I had experienced bouts of depression before, and I was there again. How on earth could I get necessary prenatal care and other necessities a baby required with no job and no money? I was over the edge–and I looked it. I had that look in my eye of instability. For years, I had worked as a litigation paralegal and expert witness, an often-stressful career, but I knew that in this condition no one would dare hire me. Right now I couldn't get a job if I had wanted to, and I didn't know if I could really count on my new boyfriend, the father of the baby I carried inside of me.

Then, on February 5, my phone rang. It was my mother, telling me that my father had died suddenly and unexpectedly. Damn her, I thought. I hadn't even known he was sick. Why did she, of all people, have to be the one to call? I hated her. To avoid seeing her, I didn't even attend the funeral. I felt I had no closure with the father I loved so much. And I never had the opportunity to tell him that a granddaughter was growing within me. Three days later, I married the father of my child. Had it not been for him, I might well have taken my own life.

With his support, I could now think more clearly. Not knowing what else to do about the taking of my son, I called the FBI since my mother had taken Zachary across state lines. What I found out next would eat at my soul for years to come. I had a child support arrearage action filed against my ex-husband in Alabama. My mother had intervened in the action by filing a Motion for Temporary Custody of my son, without serving me with notice of having done so. A hearing was set and because I was not informed of the action, I didn't appear in court. The judge, a personal friend of mine, had no choice but to grant her motion pursuant to statute. She alleged that I was an unfit mother–all because she hated the Jewish man who had come into my life. She called my ex-husband and told him that if he would not contest her custody request, she would not make him pay child support anymore. Of course, he quickly agreed and never even showed up in court.

The craziness didn't stop there. As ridiculous as it sounds, my mother told my son that Jews liked to marry Christian women who had children so they could sell the children in Iran for slave labor. My son, fearing he would be sold for slave labor, was petrified to return home.

An embittered and expensive legal battle took place over the next eight months, with my mother claiming I was not fit to be with my son. But I was a fit mother. I loved my son with every breath in my body. He was my life. After waiting months and months for a trial, the judge finally ordered my mother to return my son to me. Because state lines had been crossed, however, his return had to be processed by the State of Alabama Department of Family and Children Services. Weeks went by and nothing happened. They said they had hundreds of cases of greater urgency than mine and that Zachary would be returned when they had time to process the paperwork.

Several years earlier, I had worked for an Alabama attorney and had become intensely involved in Alabama politics. Desperate for help, I decided it was time to call on some of the powerful leaders and lawmakers I had worked so hard to help. I wrote to Hillary Clinton, explaining the inaction of the Department of Children and Family Services, begging for help. A week later I received a call from Bill Clinton's presidential aid, Bruce Lindsey, and then the president's general counsel, Bernie Nussbaum. With their help, the director of Alabama's Department of Children and Family Services soon called and let me know that my son would be home in a few days. I was so grateful for their help and at the same time so outraged that it took efforts of such great magnitude just to enforce a judge's order.

Zachary had been gone nine months and the transition was rough. When he had left, he was the only child of his newly divorced mother. He returned to a new stepfather and pregnant mother, and he was still scared that he might be sold in Iran for slave labor. Just a month later, my daughter, Jessica, was born.

She brought joy to all of us and became the constant companion of my son and an invaluable aid in his transition.

As a consequence of the kidnapping and the emotional turmoil we had experienced, our family did have some issues to work through. But without my mother in my life now, I began to experience comparative normalcy for the first time ever. A fog of dysfunction was lifting, and for a change I could see my feet, planted firmly on the ground. I was never going back to that place again, I told myself. At last, it seemed that life was rolling along and the grass was green.

I had no idea at the time that I was about to embark upon an amazing spiritual journey, one that would change my life forever. I was about to learn that God's plan did indeed work in mysterious ways. That without bumps in the road, one's soul would not grow. And that the rougher the bumps, the greater the growth.

CHAPTER 3

A Visit to the Other Side

It had been almost three years since I last worked and I decided it was time for some intellectual stimulation. Zachary was now ten and Jessica was two. I decided to work on a contract basis as a litigation paralegal so that I could still be home with my children. I had taken a job in which I would be testifying as an expert witness regarding some specific financial information. Never having done this before and knowing there was no room for error, I burned both ends of the candle for several weeks preparing for the trial, staying up late into the night.

On one of these nights, I had just settled into bed when I was suddenly aware of someone standing at the foot of the bed. It was my father. My first thought was, "What are you doing here? You are dead." I knew this wasn't a dream. I knew he was there in the room with me.

"Well, sometimes when a person dies and has something important that needs to be taken care of, they can come back," he responded. "I didn't get to tell you that I loved you."

It was strange to me that he never moved his lips while speaking to me. I just seemed to understand what he wanted me to understand. But it was more than just understanding. It was if

I knew volumes of information for each thought he had.

"I also wanted to tell you that I didn't raise you right," he said.

"What do you mean? " I said.

"Well, there is no burning hell," he said, pointing over my left shoulder. I turned to look at what he was pointing at. Just behind me was what appeared to be an invisible barrier that separated the two of us, who were standing in a place of light, from an infinite, black vastness. It was so black. There was not one star or one pinpoint of light. It was so cold that it was hot, similar to dry ice but much more extreme. There was also one soul pressed against the barrier and I could feel the emotions of this soul. I had no idea of the significance of this one soul, if this was the only one or just the only one I could see, but the feeling was unbearable. I sensed from this soul the feeling of hitting rock bottom in life–multiplied by a billion.

The soul was absolutely miserable beyond human comprehension. However, I understood that this soul was only there because he felt he belonged there. All he had to do in order to be in the place where we were, was to change his line of thought and believe: "I am there–I am in the light of God," but this soul did not know that. He only "wanted" to be in the light of God and therefore he got exactly that–the desire of "want" to be in the light of God. I understood that the concept of hell was what a person thought it would be. I intuitively understood that the emotion you die with is the emotion you carry with you when you cross over and therefore I saw the importance of dying in peace. Once crossed over, it is much harder to change your line of thought.

Being in pure spiritual form, all feelings are much more intense. Without the buffer of the human body to desensitize the emotional feelings, it is harder to find your way to the light of God. That is why hospice, special care and support for the dying and their families is so important. It is imperative that we, as loving, spiritual beings, help those who are dying with fear to die instead with peace and love. If they don't find peace and love before crossing over, they could literally be stuck, searching for the light of God. The light of God doesn't evade. The light awaits all, but the soul must understand that it needs to go there.

CHAPTER 4

The Lessons of Life and Spiritual Advancement

Next my father directed my attention to what appeared to be an organizational chart reflecting the levels of spiritual advancement of souls, with the oneness of God at the top. (I use the term God to represent that higher power, that Oneness of All, which has been given many names.)

"The life lessons you learn while on Earth determine where on this organizational chart you come in when you die," said my father, pointing at this chart. "Your lifetime on earth has life lessons attached to it. He explained that with each life lesson you have three choices: do nothing, make the positive choice or make the negative choice. The positive choice may not always look like the best choice to make. You must be careful to make the decision with the right motive and intent. It is very important to assess the motive and intent behind every single decision you ever make because that is what will determine if you learn the life lesson or if you must repeat it. Each time you make the wrong choice, the consequence will be stronger and harder to bear.

For example, he explained, it's like the teenager without a driver's license who sneaks the car out and gets caught by his parents. The parents ground the teenager. A few days later the teenager takes the car out again, except this time the teenager gets caught by the police, gets ticketed and gets grounded. A few weeks later, the teenager takes the car again, except this time, he has a wreck, gets ticketed and gets grounded. A few weeks later, the teenager takes the car again, except this time he has a wreck, someone is killed and he goes to jail with severe charges. How many times does the teenager have to be faced with the lesson before he learns not to take the car without a license? I suddenly understood the idea of life lessons and how easy it can be to determine these life lessons, how easy it would be to learn our lessons the first time... learn them and move on, without all the havoc of having to repeat the lessons over and over.

I also realized that life is like college—you choose the class you want to take and sign up—and that life lessons involve emotions attached to intent: love, hate, trust, patience, narcissism, greed, lust, pain, deceit, desire for money, and on and on. The soul must understand the entire concept of its life lesson before it can pass the class and move on. It is not necessary to experience the pain of the life lesson in order to learn it. It is entirely up to you. I was shown that the easiest way to begin this practice is to live every moment of your life by treating others exactly as you want to be treated, no matter how they have treated you. That is their responsibility. This includes things like how you treat the driver who seems to inappropriately pull out in front of you in traffic. For all you know, that driver is on the way to a dying child or just left an abusive spouse and didn't notice you were there. "Each life lesson you learn advances your soul another level," said my father. Now I understood that the lessons we learned in each lifetime are predetermined with a peer review with our soul group. With this group, we decide what lessons would benefit our soul and then we choose a life experience where we can learn those lessons. The tougher the lesson, the greater the opportunity to learn. It helped me to realize that my life lessons were not forced on me and that I had chosen them just as everyone else chooses theirs–and that the troubles we experience do have a purpose. Owning up to these lessons and responsibilities is what advances us as spiritual beings. I also realized that to know a life lesson was also to know what it was not. If you choose a life lesson that involves hatred or oppression, how would you know what they really were if you did not know what they were not? You would have to live a lifetime of oppression and hate to experience for yourself how it felt to be hated and oppressed. Lives of misfortune are not random; they are a choice and each lesson brings us one step closer to the Oneness of God.

CHAPTER 5

The Pain of the Life Review

My father then gave me a powerful analogy for life. He said that life is like a phonographic record. It spins and spins and spins. He said life is also like a movie. The actors and the plot remain the same, but the outcomes change depending on the choices the actors make. When your soul crosses over to the other side, you meet with your soul group and determine what life lessons you need to learn, choose a lifetime and body to accomplish the goal, and jump onto the spinning record of life. A soul group is a group of souls housed together through eternity to facilitate life lessons and ascension.

I understood that the bodies and things of reality remain the same; only the stories change. Physical reality is experienced in all dimensions at one time because physical reality is in fact, not real. It is atoms vibrating at a certain speed. Every single thing in the universe is made up of atoms, so every single thing vibrates. You probably learned in grammar school science that an atom is approximately 5% mass. If one atom is 5% mass, then all atoms are 5% mass. If all atoms are 5% mass, then everything you see in physical reality is 5% mass, including you. Multiple universes are experienced by the existence of the soul on many dimensions of reality at one time. It is happening and experienced as one existence by you in your life as you know it, though your soul is experiencing many lifetimes at one time. I describe it like an octopus. The consciousness of the source of all there is, or God to me, is the head of the octopus. The head of the octopus exuded energy from every angle just like the sun. This octopus has an infinite number of legs and the legs are infinitely long. These legs are hollow and the light of the source of all there is shines through the hollowness of the legs. At the end of each leg is a puppet... Easter Bunny, Barney and Santa Clause and we all know puppets can't think. What if I told you the brain didn't think and that me, you and everyone you know is a puppet at the end of a leg? The brain contains no mechanism in which to "think." The brain is a processor for information transmitted electromagnetically from the source of all there is to you. Therefore, every single event in your life is determined by source. So whatever happens is good and is exactly what your soul needs to grow. It is the manner in which you deal with the lesson that determines if emotional pain will be inflicted. I understood that bodies are simply tools to facilitate life lessons, and because a soul has to experience life while it is contained in a body, the soul is greatly desensitized. Just as your sense of touch would be limited if you tried to pick up or touch a rose petal with a glove on your hand, so a soul contained in a body cannot feel with the true intensity of its spiritual being.

As I watched this spiritual phonograph record, I understood that the motive and intent with which you do something determines whether or not you incur karma, what goes around comes around. The ultimate lesson of incarnating on this earth is to treat every single person, in every single encounter throughout your lifetime, in the same way you want to be treated, with agape, unconditional love and forgiveness. It doesn't matter whether the encounter is a fleeting moment with a passerby, or a relationship with a loved one. Every encounter matters equally.

All souls, I learned, go through a life review in the afterlife. During this review, the soul, now unconfined, will feel every single feeling that it caused every single person ever encountered, as a result of its behavior while incarnated. This includes the feelings of emotion of all those who were indirectly harmed as a result of the soul's behavior. I understood that there is a ripple effect to our actions, which eventually affect hundreds if not thousands of people, in other words, affects the entire mass consciousness of the world. For instance, let's discuss the woman who pulled out in front of you earlier. Let's assume that you were kind to her and did nothing inappropriate. She goes on her way to the emergency room to be with her dying child. Because she encountered positive energy from you, she thanked the surgeon for doing his best. The surgeon touched because he had a child at home about the same age goes home and hugs his wife with gratitude and they both put their arms around the child. The child loves the dog, the dog goes next door and nuzzles the baby over there. The cycle never stops. However had you sent negative energy, she would have arrived at the emergency room, screaming at everyone in sight. Cursing the doctor because he was such an idiot. By now its very late and he is tired. He goes home and bitches because dinner is cold because he forgot to call and say he was late. The wife takes it out on the child and you know the rest of the story. Everything you do effects the energy of the entire world. Because the soul can feel in pure form all the pain it caused others to feel, directly or indirectly, the life lesson review can be a terribly painful experience. The pain you can suffer in your life review is unlike any pain you will ever know here. However, in the same way, the positive behavior that a soul puts into effect during its life entitles it to experience intense happiness and love.

CHAPTER 6

The Volumes of Knowledge

For some reason, I took notice of my surroundings for the first time. I was in a huge room with rows and rows of what appeared to be very large books, each approximately three inches thick, which my father referred to as "volumes of knowledge." I also saw three comfortable chairs placed around a coffee table. One of the volumes of knowledge was on this table, and as I reached to pick it up my father told me not to touch it because it was "for them." I understood "them" to be souls who had crossed over, not souls like myself who were visiting, and that they used these volumes of knowledge to glean information about their lives and lessons. I later learned that the volumes of knowledge are known as the akashic records. These volumes looked somewhat like laptop computers except that to see the screen you didn't have to open it up. The screen was on the top and the soul simply touched the screen to automatically access the knowledge it sought. The information was transmitted to the soul by electromagnetic energy. (Which I could write hours about in itself but I need to stay focused here.)

I asked my father if I was doing everything I needed to do to get where I needed to go.

"Yes," he answered.

"Well, is there anything I need to do that I'm not doing?"

"Of course."

"Well, what is it?" I asked.

"I can't tell you that," he replied. "You must make those choices. They are your decisions to make. You have free will to choose what it is you do, but I will tell you this…"

Ironically, what he revealed next is the only thing about his visit that I simply cannot remember, except that I felt positive about what he said.

I then asked him if he had seen my great grandmother, who had passed when I was in the ninth grade, and he said yes. I asked if he had seen my grandmother and great-grandfather (both his relatives) and again he said yes. Then I asked if he had seen my grandfather on my mother's side and he said, "No, but I know he is here. "What is going to happen to my mother?" I asked next. Clearly, she had led a life that had caused pain to all in her destructive path and I was curious what would happen to her when she died. Though my mother was indeed assisting me in lessons I requested to learn, she could have taught me the lessons she had to teach me without being so vicious, mean and abusive. She used inappropriate methods to teach me, therefore she caused ill feelings which would result in negative karma. She chose the wrong teaching method to teach me. She could have chosen a kind method to teach me… that was her choice, which would ultimately result in negative karma for her. My father told me that she would die within the next few years, but he was not certain what would happen because it would depend on the choices she made throughout the remainder of her life.

He then said, "Well, I have to go, and I won't be back." "I just needed to tell you that I loved you." Then he disappeared and I awoke.

Over the next two years, my mother and I somewhat mended our relationship. I had grown and now understood boundaries, which I readily applied to the mending relationship. I set boundaries and guidelines as to acceptable and expected behaviors from her. She even finally called the judge (who was a personal friend of mine) and told him the truth about why she took Zachary to begin with. Simply, she had wanted him.

My mother died a few years later, just as my father had told me she would, but she died with a daughter by her side, sorry to see her go. There were still repressed hurts inside me, but they were pushed deep inside to allow the relationship to mend.

CHAPTER 7

My Spiritual Awakening

The next morning when I woke up, I had an unbelievably detailed understanding of the afterlife, souls, life lessons, humanity and karma. I also "knew" several people I had not known before I went to sleep that night. It is hard to describe the intuitive knowing of someone you don't know. The best definition I can think of is to say I knew their resonance. I knew their spiritual vibrational frequency. I knew the resonance of their soul's vibration as if it were a family member. Once I actually met them, it was if I had always known them. Once connected, we had long awaited conversations that enthralled us all.

Right away, I found that I could suddenly talk to people and instantly know the life lessons they were attempting to learn and what issues needed to be addressed in order for them to learn those lessons and move on. But I had doubts. I doubted this sudden gift. In fact, I felt as though I might be losing my mind. I worried that the events surrounding the kidnapping of my son and the stress of the impending trial had finally caught up with me and that I had lost it. Had I dreamed this event? Had I made it up in my head? Or had some higher power placed it in my head?

I had not been in Atlanta long and I didn't have any friends or other people with whom I could discuss this bizarre event. Not knowing what to do, I decided to seek out information through the only source I knew–books. But I didn't know what to read. I didn't even know what to call what had happened to me or if there were others who had similar experiences.

Feeling burdened and obsessed with this experience, I got into my car and started driving, not really knowing where I was going but just hoping to stumble across something to guide me. I ended up getting lost in downtown Atlanta and stopped in a parking lot to ask for directions. I found myself sitting directly in front of a new age bookstore. I was totally unprepared for what I found inside. I saw strange people wearing strange clothing and smelled strange incense burning. As the Baptist in me came out, I thought, What on earth am I doing in this cult store? Having worked in litigation, I tend to be a very analytical, black-and-white sort of person and this was just not on my list of normal. I was unable to attach any sort of logic to this curious incense-burning bookstore.

I decided to look around anyway. I read titles of books that were equally strange to me, books about channeling, astral travel, reincarnation, mantras, meditation and near-death experiences and randomly selected a handful of books to buy. At this point, I had no idea why I was buying the books. The first one I read was about channeling, which seemed as preposterous as my teaching a class in physics. I saw books by Dannion Brinkley and Raymond Moody–the people I had woken up having knowledge of. It is hard to explain the familiarity with these people… I just recognized them. I didn't recognize them visually, I recognized the essence of their souls. It can be described much like deja vu.

Both of these people, it turned out, were experts in near-death experiences. Dannion had been struck by lightning and had a significant near death experience and Raymond was his physician during this time. Raymond also happened to be researching near death experiences and was, and still is probably, the most significant expert in the field. The information and experiences they described from their near-death experience was far greater knowledge than anything available on this earth. What they talked about was similar to what I had experienced, except I hadn't had to die to learn about it. I was amazed to find that one of Dannion's books described how he, too, had seen the strange computer.

CHAPTER 8

The Importance of Peace for the Dying

After reading Raymond's and Dannion's books, I finally began to accept that what had happened to me was real and that I had not made it up in my head. I also learned about hospice from Dannion's book, so I realized that what my father had told me about the importance of helping people go through the process of their death was not a mistake either.

I had always wanted to work with the sick and dying but I wasn't willing to change career paths and return to school. It seemed like too much sacrifice and work. But with my father's visit and then Dannion's book, I felt it somehow had a place in my life. A few months later, I noticed an ad for hospice volunteers in a local publication and the flag went up. I was willing to volunteer but not to type or file. I wanted to work with the dying. When I called the hospice office and the volunteer said, "We just need people to be there and listen to the patients and their family members," I immediately signed up.

I have always been extremely sensitive to the emotions of others, to the point that it feels as if I am taking on their feelings. I learned from Dannion's books that a word existed for what I felt and that he had the same feelings. We were empaths. I hadn't realized that this feeling had a name or what to do with the gift I apparently had. In fact, I had never acknowledged it as a gift.

What I found was that many of the terminally ill people were afraid to die and too angry to talk about it. They were making their last days miserable for both themselves and their loved ones, not to mention the fact that they would not be crossing over in peace, which is so important. I could feel their fear as if it was my own and, more importantly, I understood why they were so afraid of death. So I would tell them of my experience with my father and my visit to the other side. When we finished talking the people were grateful, they no longer feared impending death and they could die in peace. My work also helped the family members, who came to realize that, although life was going to be different, they were not going to lose their loved one. The loved one, I told them, would still be "alive" and could even be communicated with.

One of the patients I worked with was dying of Alzheimer's and her daughter, a woman about my own age, was very angry. She could not accept the fact that her mother was dying. She would talk to no one and was withdrawing from life with her family. When the hospice office gave me her phone number, she wouldn't even return my calls. I kept calling until she finally talked to me just so I would stop calling. When I spoke, there was silence on her end of the phone. Once we spoke though, we had many more conversations over time.

Then one day as I was driving down the road, I had the impulse to call her. I felt she was in great pain. I dialed the number, asked to speak to her and was told she was at a funeral. The next day she called saying, "Eva, my 13-year-old niece died yesterday by drowning and I wanted to thank you so much for everything you have told me. I was able to share it with my sister, who is in great grief, and she was so grateful. My sister thought she saw my niece the day of the funeral and now knows that she really did see the child. Knowing that her daughter was really okay, she was able to find peace."

From that moment on, my friend was like a sponge, wanting to know everything I could possibly tell her regarding the afterlife. When her mother finally did pass, she was able to accept her death without feeling a total loss. She knew her mother was not gone forever.

Now I began to understand one of the purposes of my father's visit–my experience could help people. Those who are dying sometimes needlessly hang on for long periods because of their fear of death. It is painful for them as well as loved ones who witness the fear and grasping for life. The knowledge that life does indeed continue, that there is no need to fear this continuation and that there is no eternal damnation, could help bring both the dying and their loved ones great peace.

I also realized how much the kidnapping had changed me. Because my mother had kidnapped my child, I had been unable to be there for my father's death. Because I had not been able to be there for my father's death, he returned to see me ultimately bringing me a wonderful gift. Had I been there for his death, he would not have returned to see me, ultimately changing my entire life. My father and I were so close, I had always said when my father died I would become a hermit. I had not become a hermit at all, in fact, I had evolved into a better person. Had he told me the things he told me while he were still alive, I would never have understood what he was talking about. When I look back, I can see times when he was trying to share it, but I didn't understand what he was talking about. The depth of the material evaded me because of my ignorance. I wasn't the same person I had been before. I had evolved tremendously, both emotionally and spiritually. I believe that if my father had tried to show me these things without the growth I experienced through the kidnapping of my child, the entire experience would have meant nothing to me. It would have been fruitless. I simply would not have comprehended the magnitude of what he was trying to tell me. It was crystal clear that the bumps in the road were put there for a reason.

CHAPTER 9

The Synchronicities Begin

A synchronicity is a coupling of several significant events happening in your life near or about the same time. The American Heritage Dictionary meaning for synchronicity is a:

> *Coincidence of events that seem to be meaningfully related, conceived in Jungian theory as an explanatory principle on the same order as causality.*

Synchronicity in your life is a telltale sign that something is up with your life and your spirituality. If you become aware, and you can, of these synchronistic events, you will gain great insight and personal power. Synchronicities are green lights indicating Go, you are on the right path. The synchronicities are blatantly obvious once you start paying attention. If you are experiencing chaos in your life, take the time to look for synchronicities. It can stop the chaos.

A significant synchronicity in my life has to do with the birth of my third child. When I was in my twenties, everyone at the courthouse in the small town where I worked visited a particular psychic woman, Dorcas O'Brien, who was allegedly, amazingly accurate in her readings. At first I was skeptical about seeing her because I didn't believe in psychics. I soon learned though that everyone was right, she was very accurate in her readings. When my son was kidnapped, I desperately wanted to hear that he was coming home so I tried to contact her. But her phone number had changed. Having a background in litigation, I had always been able to find anyone, but I could not find her. I searched for months to no avail.

My mother died in June of 1998 and I was sitting out front on the curb of the funeral home in Alabama, talking to an old friend. He told me that he had gotten divorced, commenting that his wife had gone to see a psychic woman and had made a tape recording of their session. The psychic told her to take good care of the tape because that is how he would find out she was having an affair, which is exactly what happened. Anyway, we chatted a few more minutes and I said, "Well, come to Atlanta sometime, bring your kids, meet my family and we'll go rafting or something." He reached in his pocket and handed me a business card. When I flipped it over, he said, "So sorry, I didn't mean to give you that card–it belongs to that psychic woman my wife went to see." All I could do was stare at the name on the card. The name on the card was "Dorcas", the name of the woman I had been looking for all those months. I could see from her address that she lived in a rural area near Birmingham, but I didn't have the time on this trip to get in touch with her. The next time I come to Birmingham, I thought, I've just got to see her.

I returned in November to retrieve some things my mother had left me and planned to stay with my brother at his new house, which I hadn't seen before. When I got there, I realized that the psychic woman lived right across the street. Now I knew I had to see her—I was meant to see her. I made an appointment and went over to her house. "Oh, you are pregnant," she said to me as soon as I walked in the door.

"Hardly," I replied, "and I have no plans to be. In fact, I am getting my tubes tied in the summer after the charity benefit that I am working on is over."

"Well, I tell you what," she said. "If you are not already pregnant and don't want to be, you'd better be very careful, because there is a soul over your left shoulder waiting to come to you. I'll tell you something else too. This child is not a life lesson. He will be bringing you a gift."

"Okay, okay", I said, "but there is not going to be a child." I left there that day thinking she had totally lost her gift.

A few months later, I was working on a charity event called American Cancer Society's Party With a Purpose. Thousands of people would be attending, and I was in charge of the silent auction. I was working so hard to pull this together that I wasn't really giving my children the attention they needed, much less my husband. My husband and I were "together" just once in the month before the event. Since I was scheduled to have my tubes tied soon, I had decided to go off birth control pills for a couple of weeks to see how I would feel being off them after my operation. Well, as the saying goes, it only takes once. Dorcas had been right. I was speechless. I couldn't believe that at 40 years old, I was pregnant with my third child.

Two months before my baby was due, I went in for a routine doctor's appointment. "Geez, Eva, your blood pressure is soaring," the doctor informed me. "Did you get in traffic or a fight with your husband?"

"No, it's been a really nice morning," I said.

"I'd like for you to walk across to the women's clinic and get your urine checked for protein," the doctor announced. "I'd do it here, but I want the results back today."

So across the street I went. The nurse who greeted me said, "So, you're here to have a baby." I said, "Uh, no, I am here for a urine test." She said, "No, you are here to have your baby." I said, "Look, you have me confused with someone else, I am NOT here to have my baby. He's not due for almost two months."

Well, the next thing I knew was that they were connecting lines and drips to induce my labor. Evidently, my doctor had told the nurse to go ahead and induce my labor because of my blood pressure, but I was completely in the dark about her decision. Two days passed and nothing, absolutely nothing, happened. Then on the evening of the second day, a little after 6:00 p.m., I went into labor. My baby was born in less than 20 minutes–on the seven-year anniversary of my father's death, almost to the minute.

As my baby grew, he would walk around saying what sounded like "noflak." I had no clue what he was saying or trying to say. Then, when he was about two years old, we were lying in bed talking one night and he looked at me and said, "I loooovveeee Norman Flack," and just smiled at me. I couldn't believe my ears. My father's name was Norman Flack. It seemed that this child just may be bringing me a gift. A synchronistic event affirming to me that everything I had encountered was indeed real and meaningful. For how on earth would a child so small know a man that had died almost a decade before he was born? I would soon learn that I had received a gift to be shared with the world. It had been beating at my door all along but I had been too stubborn to hear. I had to be convinced that it was real and my father was the only person that would ever have been able to get that through to me. I had always known my father was an evolved being, but the real meaning of evolved was unknown to me at the time. Being evolved is much more than book learning, it is being spiritually aware. Spiritual awareness comes from within, not from a book. My subconscious had recognized the signs of spiritual awareness in my father. I was not evolved enough myself to understand what was being put before me in the form of consciousness. With everything having a frequency, the consciousness of all there is has its own frequency and once experienced in physical reality, it can never be forgotten. Something happens and you are forever changed. It is a pivoting point in one's life from which there is no return. Once I recognized what my father had been putting before me all of those years, I knew what it was and what must be done with it. It is within us all, it is just a matter of remembering.

CHAPTER 10

The Puzzle Pieces Together

About five years had gone by since the experience with my father. I had found out who Dannion Brinkley and Raymond Moody were but had not yet learned who Roy Mills was–the third person I had woken up "knowing" after my father's nighttime visit. I met a new friend who invited me to go with him to his favorite metaphysical bookstore, The Phoenix and Dragon. I was stunned upon walking in the door, when Candace, the woman who owned the shop walked up and said, "You're supposed to be writing a book, aren't you?" I said, "Yes, I think so." "Well, why aren't you doing so?" she asked. I told her that I didn't know why I wasn't writing the book. I guess I was just intimidated and afraid.

She bent her head down for a moment then looked up at me and said, "Here is what you need to do," giving me instructions on how to start the book. When you finish, she said, you need to call a man named Roy Mills." Roy Mills–the name of the third person I had woken up knowing. She told me that Roy Mills had published a book called The Soul's Remembrance and that he was a friend of Bettie Eadie and Dannion Brinkley. She said Roy would help me get my book published. She said, "I think I have

Roy's book on my shelf." When we walked over to the shelf, we found that there were none left and she told me she would order a copy and call me when it came in. A few weeks later, as I was digging through a basket full of books for something to read, I found that it was I who had bought the last copy of Roy's book from her store and just hadn't realized it.

Although it was the day before Thanksgiving and I didn't expect to hear back from Mr. Mills because of the holidays, I decided to e-mail him anyway to tell him my story and then wait and see. Much to my surprise, he called me a few hours later

"What took you so long?" he said.

"What do you mean?" I asked, a little confused.

"Aren't you a dark-haired woman?"

"Well, yes."

"I've been waiting a long time for you to call. I knew a dark-haired woman was going to enter my life and we were going to work together one day. I just didn't know who the dark-haired woman was."

Roy and I talked on and off for the next couple of years. Finally, in the summer of 2003 my kids and I decided to drive down to Bainbridge to meet Roy. We spent a couple of days talking and comparing everything he knew of the afterlife, to everything I had learned. It all related. All of the information matched. In fact, I was even able to communicate with his recently deceased wife. As I was preparing to leave, he said, "You know, you need to call Dannion Brinkley. He'll help you." That name again–Dannion Brinkley. Roy then gave me the phone number of Mel Minitor, who runs LightStream Productions and is Dannion's cousin.

I didn't have the nerve to call Mel out of the blue. Though a few months later, I was standing on the soccer field with my kids and I suddenly thought, "Okay, call." I dialed the number and Mel answered the phone.

"How did you get this private phone number?" he asked.

"Well, Roy Mills gave it to me," I said. "Don't worry, I'm not a stalker. If you don't want me to call, I'll hang up."

He laughed and said, "Well, why did you call me at this very minute?"

I told him I wasn't sure and that I just had a strong urge to do so.

"Do you want to know why you called at this very moment?" he asked. "Dannion and I have been on the road for three months and we just got home. In fact, I just walked in the door. If you had called any other time, you would have gotten my wife and she would have fussed at you for calling our private number." Mel and I have been fast friends ever since. It's as if we have always known one another. Through the connection I had with Dannion Brinkley, a man I had never met, I found a great new friend and help in pursuing my spiritual path. The synchronicities continued to amaze me.

At Christmas, Mel drove into town to visit a friend. He stopped by my house on the way to drop off presents and I told him he couldn't stay long because I had to get ready for a party I was attending. I had needed a physicist to discuss some of the information I had been channeling. I called up my old friend, the one who had originally taken me to Phoenix and Dragon because he now had a girlfriend who had just received her doctorate in physics. She invited me to attend a party with her because there would be a lot of people there with similar interests. So, I was going to a party with a woman I did not know, to a home wherein I didn't even know the hostess.

"I'm going to a party too," he said. Wouldn't it be wild if we were at the same party!"

"This is Atlanta, not Aiken, South Carolina," I replied, laughing. "There are probably ten thousand parties in Atlanta the Friday before Christmas!"

"See ya later at the party!" he said as he left. To our amazement, when I arrived at the party I was greeted at the door by none other than Mel himself.

It turned out that I met the hostess of the party, Alice, again a few weeks later at an expo in Atlanta outside the room where Raymond Moody had just finished lecturing. My purpose for going to that conference was to meet Raymond. I never got to meet him that day, because I started chatting with Robyn, the woman standing next to the hostess when Robyn's cell phone suddenly rang. I heard her tell the caller that she wished she could come home, but she had to wait for her friend to finish her lecture. I offered to drive her home, only to find out she lived just a few miles from me. On the way home, I soon learned that we had both worked at the same expo in Charlotte last November and that she had been at the same Christmas party Mel and I had attended. When she told me her name was Robyn Quail, my mouth dropped open. Her daughter had been a good friend of mine since I had been about 19 years old. I had never met Robyn Quail because she lived in Atlanta while her daughter was in Birmingham. I knew instantly it was no mistake that we had been put together three separate times over three months and knew many of the same people. Robyn had been friends with Dannion and Raymond for decades. The three of them had traveled worldwide lecturing together for years. The synchronicity of these people in my life continued to flabbergast me every day that went by. Robyn and I are inseparable friends now and I know that she was placed in my life to be my mentor. She had been involved in spiritual metaphysics for decades and was wise beyond belief.

In the spring, Robyn finally took me to Raymond's house where we spent the afternoon having lunch and talking. I told my story of how I "knew" him as he too sat and listened with disbelief. We all agreed that we would eventually lecture and teach classes together as soon as time would permit.

Everything was in place now, I had met all of the people I had woke up knowing.

CHAPTER 11

Hearing the Voice of Oneness

Another event that reinforced for me once again the importance of listening to my inner promptings happened one night when an old friend came to visit. Not knowing why, I actually coerced her to visit. I was driving back from my grandmother's in Alabama and suddenly had the strongest urge to call my friend Leslie, whom I had not seen in several years. I called her and asked her to come over.

"Well, my little girl has a friend over," she hesitated and said. "They are in their pajamas and happy so we'll come another night." But that wouldn't do for me. I was adamant. I finally said, "Look, just ask her if she wants to come and call me back." About two or three hours later, when I was already in bed, she called back. We argued for a few minutes, me telling her I would get up and she saying me she didn't want to impose, but she finally made it over.

We sat up talking for hours in front of the fireplace, catching up on the years that had passed since our last visit together. At one point in the conversation, I said, "Hey, I've been learning to read tarot cards. Let me practice on you." Tarot cards are cards that have specific meanings attached to each card. Through placement of the cards selected by a person, it was alleged that great insight can be learned relative to their life. The reading of the cards she picked said, "A friend, loved one or relative is going to die and you are going to lose all of your household possessions." At that point, we both laughed and said, "Let's just put these things away."

We talked for a few more hours and I said, "Why don't you just spend the night?" Having had a glass of wine or two, she said, "OK, I don't need to drive home anyway" and we went to bed.

About 2:00 a.m. I heard someone knocking on the front door and saw a flashlight shining outside. When I opened the door, I was greeted by a policeman who asked, "Is Leslie here?" I said, "Yes, what's wrong?" He said, "Well, her house just burned down and someone died in the fire." We were stunned. Leslie had let a young man stay in her house while he was getting back on his feet after a bad relationship. He worked with her son at a local restaurant and when they got off that night about 1 am, her son had dropped him off and then left. He was there alone that night. Had her son not dropped him off and left and had Leslie stayed at home, she, her son, her little girl and her daughter's friend would all have died.

I had begun to recognize synchronicity when it knocked. When I noticed synchronicities happening in my life, I learned that I had best pay attention.

In December 2002, I started having abdominal pains, but the doctor couldn't find anything wrong. I went to the doctor for months complaining of abdominal pain. It got to the point where the only way I could find comfort was to be still. I didn't like to be still. I was an obsessive-compulsive, Type A personality, it was almost impossible for me.

It was March, 2003 by now. I had been to the mall and was driving home when I felt a spot on my mouth like I was getting a cold sore. I took some lysine and thought nothing more about it. That night about 2 am, my son came upstairs to shower. He never came upstairs to shower because he lives in an in-law suite downstairs two levels down. It was inconvenient for him to come upstairs. Besides that, it annoyed me when he came upstairs making noise while I slept. I called to him, yelling at him to turn the light off. He walked into my room to talk to me and I saw a look of horror on his face. He said mom, something is seriously wrong with you, your face is swollen twice the size of normal. I got up and looked in the mirror and was horrified to see that what he said was true. I didn't see myself. I saw a monster, my face had swollen enormously. My bottom lip touched the bottom of my chin and my upper lip touched my nose. It was unbelievable. My son rushed me to the hospital where I was admitted for several days. I had apparently suddenly become allergic to a diuretic medication that I had been taking for years. The allergy to the medication had been the source of the months of abdominal pain, a side effect of the medication. During my stay in the hospital that week, I heard for the first time that I needed to be still. I thought that it meant that I needed to take the time and write the book that had been popping into my head for so long. I didn't pay much attention to it though because I had no idea of its significance.

A few months later, in June, I had an incident in my car. My son and I were running errands and we were about to make our next stop. We were arguing about whether or not we had time to stop and visit his friend. "No, we are in a hurry," I yelled, opening the door to get out. I thought I had put the car in park but had put it in reverse instead. The car door opened, knocked me down and the car rolled backwards, the tire rolling onto my leg before my son could stop the car. As I lay on the ground, my leg wedged under the tire, I heard the words We told you to be still. If you won't be still on your own, we'll make you be still. I heard these words loud and clear. "Okay," I said in my head. "I hear you. I will be still." But be still for what I didn't know. As I lay there, blood gushing from two terrible wounds, I actually laughed out loud with the car still on my leg. My son astounded, said "are you nuts mom? Why are you laughing?"

Their plan worked, I was laid up for about three months with chronic infection from two deep wounds, all the way to the bone. I was in and out of the hospital during the next few months. My doctor even warned me that I would probably have a terrible scar that would never heal properly. Amazingly, today, there is hardly a scar at all.

Although I heard the message and made the promise, I really didn't know how I could possibly be still. I was behind in everything I needed to do. I had a three-year-old, a ten-year-old, a seventeen-year-old, a husband, a house and a job–how could I be still with so much to take care of? So, I didn't.

Well, I should have known. "They" knew how to make me be still. A few months after I had recovered from the car accident, I was in the hospital for hernia surgery, followed by another four to six weeks in bed. As impossible and ludicrous as it seemed to me, I finally realized and accepted, that someone, somewhere had something to say and I wasn't going to get any relief until I listened.

I still didn't listen though. As incredible as it might seem, I forgot about it and soon, I began to have abdominal pains again but in a different place and significant bleeding. I went to the doctor, but he could not find anything and suggested I go to an Ob-gyn. I went to my Ob-gyn, she couldn't find anything. The months went by, the pain worsened, so I went to a different Ob-gyn, he didn't find anything either.

CHAPTER 12

Discovering the Pendulum

It was May, 2003 and I sat in my kitchen, staring out the window, miserable with abdominal pain. For some reason, just out of the blue, I remembered a pendulum a woman had given me about seven years before. I fished it out of the drawer where I had thrown it. I had an idea about a chart, much like an Ouija board, but in a small circle rather than on a board. I sat down on my computer and designed the picture I saw in my head, cut it to about an 8 inch square and laminated it. Instinctively, I knew to hold the pendulum over the chart and when I did so, the pendulum began to move in a circular motion. I could tell by the weight of the pendulum which letter it was swinging to and slowly, letter by letter, word by word, it began to spell out things.

The first sentence that the pendulum spelled was that I needed to go to the doctor because I had nonmalignant uterine cancer. My first thought was, "what the heck is nonmalignant uterine cancer?" Not knowing what else to think, I immediately made an appointment with my internist and told him what had happened. I have a very close relationship with my internist and had told him about the "consciousness shift" I had experienced in detail. I told him the whole story of everything that had been happening with the uterine pain and bleeding.. We decided to get an ultrasound to see if anything showed up. The ultrasound revealed some very small cysts and fibroids so we assumed that was the problem. Happy to know the reason for my pain wasn't a serious issue, I went back to my obsession with the pendulum.

I was so obsessed with the pendulum and what was happening that it was all I could think about. I was getting answers to all sorts of questions but had no idea if they were really coming from a higher source. I worried that somehow I was making up the information. I was doubtful though, because I was asking questions I already knew the answers to, so how could I be sure? I would ask questions like "how many children do I have" or "in what city do I live"? I knew these answers before I asked. I needed concrete answers to questions that I didn't know before I would believe.

I spent several weeks of incessant obsession with the pendulum, just playing with it. Then one morning I sat down and it began to spell out something about population growth and people. All I could think of was why on earth would someone want to tell me something about population growth. I couldn't care less about that topic. Nonetheless, I wrote it down. The more I practiced with the pendulum, the faster it came. It began to come in complete sentences, spelling out topic headlines. Before I knew it, I had pages of material. By this time, the information was coming through while the pendulum swung wildly. I no longer had to wait letter by letter, it just came in sentences as long as I sat there. It got to the point that while the pendulum would swing, I would get an entire line of information in my head. Exactly like the old word processors that had a one line display instead of an entire screen. It would spin, spelling word by word, until finally I suppose my frequency raised enough that it just came into my head in a stream. (Though I didn't understand the meaning of a raised frequency at that time.) As the words grew, so did my understanding of what was happening. Everything I had been hearing in my head began to make sense. The meaning of everything that had been coming through was finally evident. The pieces of the puzzle were finally fitting together. With this information came great ability, far beyond anything I could ever have imagined. My soul seemed to open up to the universe. The messages came strong and clear now. It was clear there was a message for the world. A message that was more powerful than anything I had personally ever heard. This message to the world was that:

God is indeed real. That we are all of the same being and that life as we know it is threatened because the world is becoming consumed with violence.

My gift seemed to grow stronger everyday with practice. All I had to do was open myself up for it to come, and it came. As clear as a bell, it came.

I had never really believed in psychic powers, much less think I would have them. Psychic powers, in my opinion, were reserved for the weird, not me. Of course, now I am considered weird by my own family members.

Now it seemed that all I had to do was think a thought and

a response would come. The best I can describe it is when you have a very sudden idea that is the absolute answer to a problem you had. It comes in a silent voice like an idea.

PART II

CHAPTER 13

Michael, Seth and Thomas

It finally occurred to me to ask who it was that I was communicating with. "We are Michael, Seth and Archangel Thomas," came the response, "and we are here to provide you with information about the soul, humanity, life lessons, karma and processes for peace in the world."

Wondering if anyone else had ever had such communication, I searched on the internet for answers. I typed in the words, "channeling Michael," "channeling Seth" and "channeling Archangel Thomas." The search for Michael and Seth both produced hundreds of web sites with similar information. I began contacting some of these people and found out that they, too, had experienced spiritual awakenings like mine. I found others who had written books by "Michael" and found the incredible Seth material channeled by Jane Roberts.

I was amazed at the similarities between my information and Roberts' information, especially since I had never heard of Roberts or her material before I received mine. The material by Roberts seemed to be very advanced material to "teach the teachers," so to speak. I understood it, but I knew it was complex and difficult to understand for the average person. The material I was channeling seemed to be the same information, just dictated in simpler form so that the average person could understand it. I bought some of the Michael books and they, too, contained many similarities to the information I had received.

By now, it was September, 2003 and I continued to write down all the things that came through. I decided it was finally time to have a hysterectomy because the pain was getting unbearable, so I scheduled the surgery. The night before I was to have the surgery, I decided to use my pendulum to see if I could get information as to the outcome of my surgery. What I received was, "You are about to meet the next man in your life." As I was married, I had absolutely no idea what this meant. They said, "Yes, he has brown hair, green eyes, likes to ride horses in the mountains and is going to give you medicine to make you feel better." I had no idea who they could be talking about. It certainly didn't sound like my doctor. They said, "When you see him, ask him if you have seen him at the stables."

I waited anxiously in pre-op one day surgery looking at every man with brown hair. But none came to me. I thought, "Oh well, I guess they were just wrong about that."

Shortly after the surgery I was awakened by a man saying, "Eva, I'm Dr. Miller." Well, I didn't have a Dr. Miller. Then he said, "I'm your urologist." Confused by the word urologist, I opened my eyes and there he stood. I knew it was him. Groggily, I said, "Have I seen you at the stables?" He said, "Well, I don't know. I'm from Colorado, but I do like to ride horses in the mountains." I couldn't believe it. He said exactly what they had said he would say. He then proceeded to tell me that my bladder had been accidentally cut during the surgery and he had been called in to repair it. Because of this incident, I had to be admitted to the hospital and stay for several days. Obviously, "he gave me medicine to make me feel better."

CHAPTER 14

The Nursing Student and Medical Intuition

The evening of my surgery, a nursing student came into my room and somehow we got on the topic of spirituality. One thing I've found is that when someone is meant to hear something "they" have to say, we always get onto the topic somehow. I told her about my channeling experiences and that I had begun to do readings for people. I also told her about the experience with Dr. Miller. She asked if I would read for her. Her reading went something like this: "Do you have pain in your lower left abdomen?" She said, "Yes, but it's my menstrual cycle. I have very bad menstrual cycles." The message I received was, "No, there is something growing in your uterus or ovaries that is not supposed to be growing there and you need to go to the doctor, now! When you were little, were your parents poor and both worked all the time? Were you the oldest and had to take care of the other children and when your dad came home from work he would take his frustrations of the day out on you? She said, "Well, yes." I told her, "That is the reason you have manifested this problem. You have retained anger because you did not get nurtured the way you needed to be nurtured when you were young and you need to forgive your mother and father. They loved you and did the best they could. She almost fled from my room. Three weeks later, she called me at home.

"Eva, do you remember me? I'm the nursing student who came into your room the night you had your hysterectomy."

"Yes, of course."

"Well, you kind of freaked me out because you knew about my abdominal pain and bleeding. So that night when I got off of work, I went to the emergency room. I just want to thank you because you saved my life. I was bleeding to death and didn't know it. My fallopian tube had ruptured because I was having a miscarriage from an ectopic pregnancy. If you hadn't told me what you did, I wouldn't have gone to the emergency room. They admitted me to the hospital and did immediate surgery." Now you must remember that I wasn't even supposed to be in the hospital. I was supposed to have one day surgery and go home. Had the doctor not cut my bladder, I would have gone home. Life works in mysterious way in order for the soul to learn lessons and ascend.

Now it seemed that I was being used to assist people with health and emotion issues. I soon learned through my channeling that it is our emotional issues that are the fundamental basis of our illnesses. If the emotional issue behind the physical issue could be determined and healed, a person could prevent the manifestation of illness. The quicker the issue is determined, the quicker the healing can begin. The channeling could pinpoint the emotional issues causing illness within a matter of minutes, something that could take months or years to determine any other way.

CHAPTER 15

Contact with the Dead

A few weeks later as I sat working with the pendulum, it suddenly spelled out: "Please call Pat P. and tell her that this is John, Stephen and David and that I love and miss her." Pat was my relatively new neighbor and I didn't know her well. I thought, I'm not calling Pat and telling her that, she'll think I'm nuts. A few hours later the phone rang and I heard, "Hi, Eva. It's Pat. I wanted to know if I could come over and visit." I had not spoken to Pat in six months and here she is calling me on this particular day!

So I just couldn't help it I had to ask: "Do you know John, Stephen and David?"

There was an odd silence and she said, "Well, John was my son. David and Stephen were his best friends. Stephen is a friend in Ohio and David was driving the car the night he was killed."

"Well, you'd better come on over," I said. By the time she got there, the pendulum had spelled out: "Please also tell Pat this is Evelyn and she'll know it's me because when we were little, we played in the sandbox together and I threw sand in her eyes. I also gave her my favorite pie recipe 20 years ago and she is still using it."

When Pat arrived, I asked if she knew Evelyn. "Yes, she is my aunt," said Pat. I told her what had come through and she said, "That's right, and I cried and cried. But the recipe wasn't for pie, it was for pound cake. However, my aunt is not dead Eva. I didn't know what to think now. It seemed that now I was not only getting information from some unknown source but I was also communicating with loved ones, both dead and live. Again, I sat in disbelief.

CHAPTER 16

I'm Not Special

I'm not special. The knowledge of "hearing" is available to all of us. I cannot emphasize it enough. If I can "hear" the knowledge, anyone can. I never dreamed I would ever do anything like this. If you can daydream and if you have the desire to connect with God and all there is, you can hear. It takes time and discernment, but it is available to all who seek. It comes with certainty and clarity, you just have to trust that it is what it is.

The information is not used discriminatively. No one is more special than the other. God, the consciousness of all there is, is available to all. Anyone who asks, will be responded to accordingly. Do you not say prayers? Why not just learn to hear the answer when you say the prayer? Is it your preference to wonder if your prayers are heard or is it your preference to hear the response right away? It is your choice what you decide to do, but it is available to all.

The information has been available forever, since the beginning of time, but was discouraged because it was being misused. That is why it was written out of the biblical teachings to begin with. The knowledge is powerful and was being used to accumulate wealth, not to communicate with the source of mankind. The sages of biblical times saw that the powers were being abused and acted with their own judgment to discredit their use to protect mankind from inappropriate use. Had it not been for inappropriate use, the ability would be written in the teachings of recognized spiritual scholars today.

I describe my hearing ability like this: Go back to the time when you were a child in school. It's after lunch, your stomach is full, you are lethargic from the heat and your mind begins to wander and daydream...it is empty of thought. If you can remember how it felt in your mind when you did that...that soaring, free, fluid feeling, then you can teach yourself to hear and discern. When the information comes, it feels just like an idea. Think about how it feels when you suddenly have the perfect solution to something you have been puzzling about and you say to yourself, "Oh my gosh, that's a great idea!" That's the way it is. It doesn't come as a booming voice; it is like hearing a silent voice in your head, just like an idea. That's the best way I can describe how the information comes to me.

At first, it can take several weeks or even months between the time you pose the question and the time you receive the answer (or idea, as it might seem). Personally, I have found that with the use of my pendulum and chart my accuracy is better. Somehow as the information comes into my head, the pendulum spells it out on the board. If I get a word wrong in my head, the pendulum will stop spelling and just spin in a circle. When it does that I know I have something wrong. Either I don't have the word in my vocabulary or it is a situation of a word sounding like another word. My friends all harass me about using the pendulum, but my readings are accurate so I just leave a good thing alone. Why fix it if its not broken I say. I'll just have to look funny when I give a reading or maybe it will come with time. In any event, the more you practice posing questions and receiving answers/ideas, the easier it becomes. Before long, you will notice that you can literally have dialogues in your mind. That is how it works for me. You just have to pay close attention and discern the difference between your average daily thought and the thought of higher wisdom. Again, the more you practice, the easier it is to discern. The answers are always logical information and what you always knew but thought was your own idea. Your soul has the knowledge of all there is, so intrinsically you possess the knowledge of all there is and the solution to any problem you might face. The knowledge may come differently for some depending on your interest and awareness. When I get information, I set aside a black three dimensional box in my head. I don't allow anything to come into the black box but that of consciousness. That makes it easier to discern.

Artist and musicians may hear it through their painting or their music. But the information is the same. It is distinct and clear.

CHAPTER 17

Questions and Answers About the Afterlife

I have always had extreme curiosity about issues of the soul and afterlife. I remember when I was about fifteen, it was Christmas Eve. There were no presents under the tree and no one cared. We were not poor, just no one cared. I prayed to God, "Do you even hear me? I don't believe you do. If you do I want proof. I want that candle on my dresser to flicker in a manner that I'll know its you." Well, about 15 minutes later the candle started flickering like it was being blown by wind. It still wasn't proof though, because no one else witnessed it. So I said to God, "I want you to do it again when my dad gets home from work. I want time allowed for him to open the door, walk in and sit down and any air currents subside. Then I want the candle to do it again." It happened. After a long ten minutes or so, the candle did it again.

Once I was able to communicate with a source of higher knowledge, I decided that I had many questions I wanted to ask. I wrote out a list of every question I could think of regarding souls and spirituality. After I wrote down all of my questions, I began to receive responses.

I would take my kids to the pool and sit while they played

and work with my pendulum. The people at the pool of course, had no idea what I was doing, but always curious. Every day someone would come up and ask "what on earth are you doing, Eva?" I found that by working with my pendulum in front of people, it provided an opportunity to expose them to my work and the message I had to share. I found that there was always an interest with the people who would approach with inquiry.

One day, I forgot to take my list of questions and was amazed to find that though I did not have the list, the responses still came. Not only did they still come, but they came in the order I had written them. The remainder of the book consists of those questions and the responses I received for each of them. It is my hope that a spark of enlightenment will touch all who read this information. I have written the responses verbatim as they were dictated to me. I did not allow any editing of the dictation because I am under the impression that the words are important to be spoken just as they are, without change. So, that's what you get.

The information from Michael came first. The information provided by Seth on physical reality and manifestation that you will read later in this book didn't come until November, 2003–interestingly, the day after the Astrological Harmonic Concordance. I believe the concordance raised the frequency of all who were on the cusp of the frequency vibration. It allowed all on the cusp to move to the next level of frequency.

I had invited friends over for lunch on Saturday, the day after the Harmonic Concordance, to discuss metaphysics. It had been only about six weeks since my hysterectomy and my energy was still very low. I complained that I was afraid my "gift" had left me, but they all assured me that it was just a matter of time. Sure enough, the next day we began the session commencing with the topic of physical reality. I have to admit it frightened me to write on this topic because I knew absolutely nothing about the laws of physics or about parallel universes. In fact, I was absolutely petrified. I thought, what if what I am writing makes no sense to those who understand physics and parallel universes? I needed to talk to someone who understood physics and also believed in metaphysics—a combination that I thought would be hard to find.

My problem was solved when I found out that my new friend Robyn Quail, had a boyfriend who was a physicist. Dr. Roy Scruggs, it turned out, was not just any physicist. He had helped design and build the Apollo spacecraft at NASA. This convinced me yet again, that I was communicating with a higher source who knew I needed a metaphysical physicist and provided one. I had experienced so much, but it didn't matter, I still had a problem accepting that what was happening was real. I constantly needed confirmations. It just seemed too unbelievable to be true. Not only was Roy metaphysical, but he had also read and studied all of the Seth material channeled by Jane Roberts and knew it well. He, too, was astonished at the similarities between my work and Roberts' work. Through Robyn and Roy, I met many people who were both scientifically and metaphysically inclined. I found many credible people who discussed with me and confirmed the teachings of physics and manifestation that I was receiving.

During the fall of 2003, I began to speak around Atlanta on the teachings I was receiving and met many new people. One day I received a phone call from a man who had attended one of my lectures. He told me that he was a scientist and was writing a book about the ancient mathematics of Atlantis. He told me that he had encountered some problems with some of his analogies and would like my help in resolving them.

I literally laughed out loud and said, "My friend, you have come to the wrong person. I know absolutely nothing about your topic of interest, much less solving the problem."

"Well, please just try," he said. "You don't know what you can do until you try."

Reluctantly, I agreed and we spent about an hour on the phone. What resulted flabbergasted me. I was actually able to tell him in layman's terms the problem with his equation. I can't remember exactly what I channeled, but it had to do with the length of the universe and computing the rate at which light travels across the universe and the rate of growth in which the universe expands. He thanked me profusely and said I saved him months or maybe even years of research.

Just as what happened that day took me by surprise, I have been in awe about the information I received for this book. I have worked in litigation all my life and never thought about anything like this before. Not only was I unfamiliar with the concepts of afterlife, I thought you died and went to heaven or burned in hell, what did I know? I didn't know about souls, planes of evolution, karma and life lessons that were being given to me, but once I had received the information I knew it. It resonated within my soul and was meant to be shared with the world. If only one soul woke up, it was worth all of the effort to bring it forth into existence. For one soul at a high vibration negates a lot more negativity by lower vibrations. The material that follows discusses at length the life of the soul, humanity, the dimensions of reality, mass consciousness, the incredible power of thought and the manifestation of physical reality and health.

CHAPTER 18

The Origin and Existence of the Soul

How do souls come to be?

Souls were originally one with God, the ultimate energy. Imagine a piece of God, flung out into the universe without knowing all there was, all there is and all there will ever be. That is how souls begin. They then need nurturing to learn and grow. They experience many lifetimes and have spiritual guides that stay with them throughout these lifetimes. The knowing or remembering the soul has of these guides is taken away and it is up to the soul, through free will, to remember and hear the voices of their teachers, for that is our entire purpose for being here.

A soul is then born into a baby's body and grows to an adult. Once a soul is born into a baby's body, God takes away the knowing. If the soul is not an old soul, it can enter the baby's body anytime it decides it does not want to return to the womb of God. If the soul is an old soul, it will enter the body at about six months in order to prepare for being confined again. Once the soul enters the body, it can leave only in astral travel and dreams or the body will die.

During this process, it learns much about life and begins

its karma. Essentially karma is that you do to others what you want done to yourself, and therefore in your next lifetime, you are treated the same way. It is the conscious action of kindness and love or lack thereof, that can change the world.

Within each lifetime, the soul has experiences that can cause it to wake up to knowing. These experiences are best described as consciousness shifts. The soul has the opportunity to receive much knowledge and when it reaches a certain level of knowing, it can ascend to higher levels of awareness.

How many lessons do we usually have in a lifetime?

Each soul chooses about nine life lessons for a lifetime and when the soul dies, it meets with a teacher for each of those lessons. The lessons learned and those that remain to be learned are reviewed during the intervals between lifetimes.

Do we always have to learn by experiencing the pain of life lessons?

Souls can also grow through guidance of other souls. In fact, they can learn more by observing other souls' experiences, such as occurs in a school classroom. However, it is much harder to learn this way because deep awareness is needed and much focus is required. With the "knowing" taken away during incarnation within a body, it is much harder to find that knowing. Once it is found, it is hard to accept the knowledge for what it really is. A tendency exists to believe that you made up the knowledge in your head, though if thought about and pondered, the knowledge is logical, because it is what it is.

How many times have you been told something is not

good for you but do it anyway? You act like you didn't hear the words, but you did. You do that to us all of the time. You hear us, but pretend you don't and then continue on with your journey seeking. We've never quite figured that one out.

The body is like a glove. As wonderful and phenomenal as a body is, it has great limitations. Imagine feeling a delicate rose petal while wearing a glove. That is how the soul experiences the knowing that was taken away. It is there, but it is hard to feel while wearing the glove of the body. It takes practice and imagination to form the knowing of how the delicate rose petal would feel if you could only touch it without the glove. Each tiny, fine line contained within the petal must be studied closely.

It is no different in learning to feel and recognize the knowing. Study your consciousness closely. Many lifetimes of learning are imbedded within the cells of your body and mind, all which contain the knowing of your origination. The voice is quiet and still, but it is there–the voice of your origination, the ultimate energy and knowing of the Oneness.

Speaking of the mind… just what is the mind? The mind is the psyche of the soul and the psyche is the container for "all that is" of that particular soul. The psyche is different for each soul depending on the lifetimes experienced by each soul. The psyche is intangible as to weight, but carries great weight as to the existence of the soul. The psyche can be measured by the depth of knowledge one has of the afterlife and of other life forms. Knowledge of other life forms is indicative of the psyche's ability to access the content of its deepest knowledge.

The psyche is stored in the aura and chakras of the physical body. The psyche is controlled by electromagnetic energy and can be stimulated to access the contents of the soul's existence. The psyche is connected to the soul's akashic records to which information is added by electromagnetic impulse.

A consciousness of One is all there is. For a consciousness of One has no separation. The separate states of mind are only a figment of your imagination. A consciousness of one experiences all there is at one time.

I understand the concept, but cannot imagine how it is felt.

Well, it goes like this. The mind is a multi-part machine. It both receives and transmits at the same time. As it awaits receipt of information to process, it can communicate with other dimensions of your higher self. Therefore, it lives many lives at once through extensions of Self. So really, you are the figment of Self's imagination, not your own.

Who is Self?

"Self" is all there is and you are a figment of Self's imagination and Self is the name of all there is.

Self is also the imagination of everyone else since self made the imagination of everyone else. See, we are all one, inside out.

CHAPTER 19

Population Growth and Young Souls

Many young souls are born every day. They are easy to recognize, for they are the ones who cause anger and violence. They teach hate through their behavior. Population growth causes young souls to incarnate without the necessary preparation, causing more violence and anger within the world. Rampant population growth fosters crime and violence and destroys the earth. If problems associated with population growth are not addressed, younger souls will overtake the older souls and cause much chaos within the world. Older souls are the providers of wisdom and are necessary elements for peace.

One of the problems is that souls need at least nine earth years between lifetimes to prepare for the next incarnation. Before they are born into the world, they have to learn dignity, grace, kindness and patience or they will be born with anger and violence. The reason for this is because it starts out as a mass of atomic matter. The atomic matter is made by defined chaos. Once the boundaries of the chaos have been determined it then needs to be exposed to the womb of God for its life force. Without life force there would be no force to push the chaos into reality. The speed with which souls are incarnating due to overpopulation is not allowing for this learning to occur.

CHAPTER 20

The Origination of a Soul

When a soul is created, the "knowing" of God is taken away and they are ignorant. They do not originate in the light of God; they are born in darkness in the womb of God, as was God.

A soul begins as a mass of energy, minus the knowledge of God. God made the light, he opened the way. Souls follow after God. Souls find the light of God and learn dignity, grace and love. They learn by example from spending time with God. They learn these things before ever incarnating and the current population growth does not allow this to occur. Souls are incarnating without the skills they need and this is causing great chaos. This rapid incarnation causes souls to incarnate early, threatening humanity with violence and chaos. Because young souls are incarnating without proper preparation to obtain the skills they need, they are inhibited from functioning properly and are unable to act in accordance with God's standards. They act without dignity, grace, patience and, ultimately, without love towards one another. Can't you see that modern humanity treats their peers worse and worse as time goes by? That is why modern society should slow down because when you slow down, you can see what you are passing by.

Souls need proper guidance before incarnating. Before

incarnating they need much teaching regarding love, for they are like babies. They need to be taught much and will grow accordingly. A soul needs time to do these things and the current population growth does not allow for this to occur. Through awareness, people can change this problem.

The overpopulation problem needs to be addressed so that young souls can mature. There will be no need for the universe if all of the anger and violence doesn't stop. The Oneness of all there is, of which we are merely extensions, is growing weary of the anger and violence, and the time is upon you to take the necessary steps to save the earth and mankind. We are all one, a part of God, the ultimate Oneness; and if the majority grows tired and weary of the anger and violence, then all there is grows tired and weary of the anger and violence. We must all make the effort for peace in the world. We are certain it can be done or we wouldn't spend this time writing this book with Eva. We are certain that humanity can be saved if the people want it to be saved.

But I thought that God didn't take life into his own hands. I thought life was free will.

Well, you must remember that we are all one. We are all extensions of God. Therefore, if God is weary of negativity, it means that the consciousness of the masses are weary–because the masses, individually and jointly, are extensions of God. So basically, all there Is is growing weary of the violence and negativity.

What we mean by consciousness of the masses is exactly

what you experienced when the world trade towers were assaulted by terrorists. The entire world grieved. The cities unknown to one another grieved. The churches prayed, the people as a whole prayed. All were affected by the attack. Just as all were affected by the attack, all are affected by the violence worldwide. It is this affect that we are trying to describe.

Hate and violence starts in the individual homes, under your very eyes, under your own roof, with your own children. Where else do you think it starts? Then it moves to the schools and businesses, then the suburbs, then the towns, then the cities, then the counties, then the states, then the countries, then to the global masses. It cannot be denied for what it is, just look at your television tonight. You should now have a new understanding of what you see on your television. Things like the bombing do not happen all at once. It happens over time, be it great or be it small, it all happens over time, right under your very eyes, under your own roof, with your own children. If you do not teach your children that love is all there is, then this world is in trouble. It is the children whose lives are at stake, but it is the children who can make a difference. But it all starts at home with *you* and the way *you* raise your children. It is up to you to make a difference if you want your children to lead happy, productive lives as opposed to lives filled with misery; and don't think for one minute that time is not of the essence. You have about six or seven years to implement structural changes before it is too late. It is our hope that you hear this message loud and clear, for if you don't, it is your own lives at stake.

For peace to come, all souls must feel love. For a soul cannot exist without feeling loved. A soul must love as well; it cannot exist without loving. If a soul desires to feel love, it will give love. If the love given is not received and the soul does not feel loved in return, it will forget its memory of how love feels. If a soul forgets its memory of how love feels it will breed negativity due to an accumulation of electrons. Love is the essence of life and all souls seek it. Love is the only source of food for the soul and the single nutrient needed by the soul. Love has everything a soul needs to grow and develop. Without it, when incarnated, a soul becomes needy and even violent at times. Love is the single most important need of a soul. Without love a soul feels nothing but emptiness and will incur much negative karma and never become one with God.

CHAPTER 21

Free Will and the Role of the Archangels

If God is all-knowing and knows that without preparation a soul will be born with anger, why doesn't he just fix the problem?

God, the ultimate energy, is indeed all-knowing and can do all things, but God does not play with life or interfere with free will in the physical dimension. Free will is a tool given for souls to learn lessons while in physical reality in order to ascend, to ultimately reunite with the Oneness. In physical reality without free will (choices), there would be no mechanism with which to learn the lessons of life. Everything is ultimately a choice with free will, a choice to do as you like. It is up to the individual to make the choice so that the changes may be implemented in the world on a mass level.

Can you tell the difference between archangels, angels and guides?

Many people need archangels in their life to survive. Archangels keep people safe from harm by intervening and protecting them from the young souls who are causing anger, violence and chaos as a consequence of incarnating too early.

How can Archangels intervene when you just said that God does not interfere with free will?

As it is right now, Archangels can intervene in one's life by answering prayers for help. When the world gets to the point of overwhelming negativity and the Archangels can no longer make a difference in the outcome of the world by answering prayers, there will be no more Archangels to intervene in the lives of the people. Because of overwhelming negativity and violence, it would take many more Archangels to save the world than there are Archangels available. Archangels are a long time in the making and take many, many lifetimes to grow and learn.

Archangels are different from regular angels in that Archangels do not have to seek permission from the higher power to facilitate change. Regular angels have to receive permission before initiating change. Regular angels have to seek permission because they do not possess enough knowledge to intervene on behalf of the masses. Archangels can intervene in events which will effect the masses, regular angels cannot.

Archangels can remove the anger from the young soul by placing love and peace in the young soul's heart before it causes harm. Young souls are particularly sensitive to love. They want to be loved and do not usually reject love given. That is another reason why it is so important to treat every person as you want to be treated. You have no idea how many people need love who do not receive it. By treating an angry, young soul with love, the heart can be softened and the anger diluted. However, some young souls need a lot more love than one archangel can give and therefore these souls need several archangels in order to act appropriately. More archangels are needed because it takes time to accomplish this and the current population growth causes deficits. People must decide they want peace and act accordingly or the world will be no more. Life as it is, is threatened. Souls are incarnating much too early and violence is overwhelming. The people of the world must make a conscious effort to treat others as they want to be treated.

Life as you know it is drastically close to changing due to a shift in the energy ratio of the earth's electromagnetic field. You do not want this energy field to shift to a negative polarity. This shift will occur in your lifetime and if negative, will make life hard to bear for those left on earth. Specifically, what we mean is, the days of happy times are drawing near. Within six years, if the vibrational frequency of the masses is not changed, there will be war on US soil for the first time in decades. The Chinese will support terrorist in the form of civil servants who will tap into security of the US government, catching the US government off guard in the form of nuclear attack in the four corners of the country. It is only through raising the vibrational frequency of the masses that this can be avoided.

No archangels will be available during that time to assist with the negativity in the world, as they will have been reunited with the Oneness. No more guides will be allowed. The people will have to make their choices without the assistance of a more evolved being. Whether or not they believe in the existence of more evolved beings is irrelevant. The fact is, they do exist and they do assist in the daily lives of the people. The people will live in despair if the violence is not stopped. If you don't know what to do, simply start by treating each and every person you meet as you would like them to treat you. That includes the person who pulls out in front of you, the telephone solicitors, the toilet janitor, the slow store clerk...everyone. Treat everyone as you wish to be treated, every moment of the day.

Can you explain if the indigo children can help counter the negative effects of the young souls?

The indigo children of the world have their frequencies ready and awake to take over where the adults in their lives leave off. These children have all been born into spiritually evolved circles of people so that they are in training so to speak for what will be presented to them. They will be ready to take the world to the next frequency if the world is ready to unite. That is why what we do now is so important.

CHAPTER 22

Karma, Motive and Intent

What is karma and exactly how does karma work?

Karma basically determines how the soul progresses through life and what its next life lessons are. Motive is behind everything. It is the motive and intent behind the action that determine karma and the life lesson. If you hurt someone with good intentions, you incur no negative karma. You incur no karma at all. If you hurt someone intentionally, you will incur negative karma and be required to pay it back in another lifetime. A soul's interaction with other souls will determine its next life lessons. It will choose the life lessons to learn and will then choose a life in which to incarnate.

CHAPTER 23

The Difference Between Karma and Life Lessons

What is the difference between karma and life lessons?

It is important to understand the difference between karma and life lessons–they are distinguishable. Karma is payback; life lessons are teachings. You can get karma in life lessons. During the learning process of life lessons if a soul creates ill feelings with another, it creates karma. It is the life lesson learned that is necessary to ascend, not the karma accrued. Life lessons are necessary to ascend, but karma is not. Life lessons have growth attached to them and karma does not. Karma is not a life lesson, but life lessons are attached to karma. For example the life lesson of betrayal. A soul can either learn the lesson of betrayal through observation of another's soul's experience, or it can experience the lesson of being betrayed. When betrayed if the soul seeks revenge and commits a vengeful act, it will incur karma. However, if it responds to the betrayal with agape, or unconditional love for another, then the lesson is learned and no karma accrued. It matters not how the other party has treated you; that is their problem to later deal with. It matters simply how you treat them, regardless of reason. Agape is the ultimate intent of the soul.

Regardless of the issue or lesson presented, a soul's ultimate goal is agape, unconditional love. Karma is consequences. Life lessons are lessons to ascend and grow.

But some terrorists believe their intentions are good!

Eva, the terrorist in the world know within them that their intent is power. Therefore, the intent behind their actions is wrong. The terrorist do not want the masses to be informed of their true intent because then the money behind their support will cease like dust in the wind. The terrorist know that knowledge is power, therefore, they attempt to keep their people ignorant of the truth. If the people supporting them knew the truth, the people supporting them would stop them.

Can karma be changed?

Negative karma will continue as long as there has been no forgiveness or desire to be forgiven. It doesn't matter if the person forgives you or not...it matters if you learned the lesson and sought forgiveness. That fact that someone might not forgive is karma creating for their own self. Agape and ultimate forgiveness is the intent of the soul. If someone desires to be forgiven and makes the effort to seek forgiveness, the karma can be absolved whether or not the other person forgives or not. The point is for the lesson or consequence to be learned and once it is learned, forgiveness to be sought.

CHAPTER 24

Suicide, There is No Escape

What about suicide? What happens when a person commits suicide?

Suicide is not a karmic issue as most think. It is a soul's escape mechanism from life. Suicide does have consequences though, in that a soul who commits suicide does not get to cross over into the light of God. A soul who commits suicide must go through a cleansing stage, a detoxification of the negative energy, which is very painful since the soul has to experience its accrued karma in pure spiritual form. This is much more painful than experiencing its karma in the body because the body is to the soul what a glove is to a hand. The body has great limitation as it relates to feeling and with the glove (the body) removed, the feeling of the soul is tremendously intensified. When the soul is incarnated things are much easier to endure, for in its original state the soul feels with an enormous intensity completely unknown to mankind.

A soul who commits suicide is just a kiss away from life. After its suicide, it will reside on the astral level. This level is not really much different from the experience of the earthly plane with the exception that only thoughts exist; there are no physical boundaries and there is no physical body. All of the pain it was trying to escape still remains.

A soul who commits suicide will experience emotional pain that is indescribable in human words and will not cross over until it resolves the pain it was originally experiencing. The reason it cannot cross over is that for purposes of growth and karma, it must resolve the pain on its own. This is not punishment. A soul must always learn the lessons of a lifetime. If it gives up to suicide and does not learn to resolve the pain on its own, it will only have to repeat the lifetime. A soul has to learn what it is meant to learn. It doesn't get to disregard the lessons. A soul will always be responsible for its lessons and life should go on until it is time to be taken away.

CHAPTER 25

Reincarnation of Souls

Souls are to people what God is to souls, each being the foundation of the other. Life is no longer so easy for souls because of overpopulation–souls are incarnating without being ready and they need archangels. Souls need time to grow and learn before incarnating and people need to understand this.

Souls are one with God before they are souls. God takes away the knowing of God and their origin, and then they are souls. Souls must desire to incarnate before they are freed of the "knowing". They are taken to a place of darkness and gradually exposed to the light of God, the ultimate energy. Once exposed, they are gradually allowed longer intervals of exposure. When they are ready, they are allowed to hear the frequencies of light and experience the warmth of love. Once experienced, they want more and more and gradually become ready to incarnate. Once ready, they meet with God for God's omnipresent love to warm them before being born into a human body. We all know how it works from there.

During the body's growth in the womb, a soul is allowed to return to the omnipresence of God as much as they like. Once the body is born and the soul incarnates, the soul is no longer allowed to return and must grow on its own. Once it interacts with other souls, its chosen lessons begin and its karma accrues. Karma begins at nil. Karma is accrued based on interaction with other souls and whether or not that interaction is positive or negative. Souls always have the ability to return to the warmth of God in between incarnations if they choose to do so. The warmth of God is not in the essence of God, it is in the womb of God.

What is the difference between God's essence and God's womb?

God's essence is different in that it is omnipresent. God's womb is only available to new souls and it is in darkness. Souls are only allowed to visit God's womb prior to incarnating. They can visit as many times as they like prior to incarnating, but after incarnating they can visit no more.

Souls are allowed to astral travel and to teach loved ones in dreams. The soul stays in the body until it dies and then it returns to God and God's essence. Then it meets with its life review committee and discusses its life lessons and the karma accrued. That takes about six months in time as you know it. Then the soul takes a rest from its recent incarnation for as much time it chooses and then goes back into the light of God for warmth and love.

What is the difference between the light of God and the womb and essence of God?

The light of God is different from the womb of God and the essence of God. The light of God is the light of healing for souls who have experienced negativity in their physical incarnation.

This light has been described by those who have had near-death experiences. Once in the light of God, the soul can stay as long as it chooses and then decide if it wants to incarnate again.

What happens if a soul decides to incarnate again?

If it decides to incarnate again, it will go to the womb of God for love and start the process all over again.

CHAPTER 26

Manifestation–The Power of Thought and the Mind–A Powerful Tool

Thought is the intent behind everything that is. It is your thoughts that put you into action when you want to get something done. Without your thoughts, what would you do, sit and stare blankly out the window? Of course that's what you would do because you wouldn't be able to think of anything else to do. So, if your thoughts place into action everything you do, what does that tell you? It should tell you that thought is a very powerful tool. So, if you have thoughts and place them with electricity and the electricity pushes them out into the world, the combination of the two is obviously very powerful. You don't doubt that electricity is a powerful source of energy do you? And you certainly don't doubt that thought is a very powerful instrument on its own. So, it is only logical that the two combined are perhaps the most powerful mechanism for accomplishment in existence. When your brain processes (mind you I said processes, not thinks, because the brain does not think. It simply processes like a computer) a thought, it sends an electrical impulse across what is called the synapse of your nervous system. This is a known fact, just ask your doctor. When the electrical impulse travels across the synapse of your nervous system, it pushes the thought on your mind out into the conscious world. If we have already established that thought and intent is behind everything you do, then we have established that thought is actually, manifestation of reality. So, when you ask yourself "How can I manifest anything I want?" You can know that it is you and you alone that has manifested your life as it is today. It is you that has manifested those things in your life that you love; and it is you that has manifested those things in your life that you don't love. It is you and you alone that allow thoughts to exist in your head. It is you that has manifested every single thing in your life as you know it. If you sit there in amazement and ask "How could I have manifested my life the way it is?" Then you should sit back and revisit every single thought you have ever had because it is those thoughts that are your life today. An example for some would be those thoughts you had when you were a teenager that you just wanted to run away with that boyfriend/girlfriend at all costs and at risk of everything you had going for you? Well, that is the thought that has brought you where you are today. Had you not ran away with that lover and had you not gotten pregnant before you got that education you were so excited about…remember? Remember back in the second grade you wanted to be a brain surgeon? There was a reason you wanted to be a brain surgeon and that reason was because you were capable of doing so. But because you changed your thoughts and your intent for life changed, you manifested a different life than you originally intended. You manifested a life in which you live month to month and day by day. You have no hopes of that bright future of retiring at the beach. You forgot to include that in your plans for your life. Your forgot to think about it at a conscious level on a regular basis; therefore you forgot to manifest it.

Manifestation is a step by step, day by day, minute by minute process and occurs over time. It is not immediate. You first place the thought and then follow the thought with action. That is all there is to manifestation. If you find you have a thought in which you do not know what action to take, then ask someone who does know. If you can't find someone who knows, then go to the library or bookstore and read. For anything you need to know can be found by reading.

All that matters is that you take the action to follow the thought. Let nothing, absolutely nothing, stand in your way. Not money, not love, not anything at all. For if you follow your life's purpose, all those things will find you. When your consciousness raises to a certain level, things just happen in your life synchronistically, requiring absolutely no action by you except to accept them.

We hope that scenario helps you to better understand manifestation.

The mind is a powerful thing and should be used wisely. Thoughts are pure energy. Compare them to electricity. You cannot see electricity, but you know it is there and you know it is powerful. Thoughts are energy, much more powerful than electricity, because thoughts are combined with motive and intent. Energy makes things happen. Energy and thoughts can be a dangerous combination because it is thoughts and negative energy that start wars. It is not the people but the way the energy is put to use. People use the energy in wrong ways. They need to make sure that the energy they use is positive.

How can you tell the difference between positive and negative energy?

You can differentiate negative from positive by determining whether or not it would cause anyone pain. Would you want the thought you are thinking about someone else to be thought about you, especially if you knew that the thought would ultimately manifest in some form? That is what happens, for the thoughts do not stay in your mind. They are energy. They go out into the universe and ultimately manifest their intent. Most people believe that a thought it is harmless, but it is not. Never underestimate the power of the mind. People need to think very carefully about what their thoughts are, because thoughts place action and energy in motion.

CHAPTER 27

Manifestation and Pollution

Now that we are talking about manifestation, people must realize that they are manifesting a trash dump. The pollution doesn't just appear; it is manifested by the people. The people want convenience, but they didn't think of what to do with the waste afterwards. Pollution is a big problem and is killing the planet. People must not pollute the planet and must be more aware of the environment. The planet will die if the pollution is not stopped and all life will cease to exist.

At the current pollution rate, how long can the planet survive?

At the current rate, the planet has about ninety years left. Please stop the pollution.

CHAPTER 28

Cellular Vibrational Frequencies and Your Health

You need to understand that the reality of your health is a direct result of the things you put into your body–both tangible and intangible. If you put unhealthy food or unhealthy energy, of whatever source, into your body, you will manifest illness. It matters equally what you put into your body and your mind, for they are the containers for your soul. If you would only understand the power of manifestation, you would understand all there is, and how it relates to everything that is. All there is, being everything in existence and everything that is, constituting life as you have created it. Manifestation is the result of everything that is, and everything that isn't for manifestation is of free will. You are in charge of your own reality.

Vibrational medicine is the wave of the future. If you want a lucrative career on the cutting edge, then you are looking at it. Cellular vibration is the foundation for all illness. It is only logical that it is what we say, just look under a microscope and tell us it isn't so. You need to pay attention to organ vibration and attached emotion of the person that needs to be fixed. If you can resolve that issue within five years, the disease, of whatever source will not manifest. These frequencies must match the frequencies of the laws of the universe in order to function properly.

By learning the cause of illness, you can have your health in your own hands. First of all every hamburger, every pizza and every salad you put into your body has a frequency. Tell us, which do you think carries the highest frequency? Okay, so you chose the salad. But how many of you are absolutely sure that the salad was chemical free of poisons?

Now, how many of you use modern electrical appliances such as cell phones and microwaves? These things breed mutation of cells within your body.

Learn about those things of which you have no knowledge such as homeopathics, vibrational medicine and natural essences. Learn to use these things and you lean to prevent illness.

Can you give me examples of how we manifest our health? Are certain emotions tied to certain parts of the body?

The vibrational frequency of your cells get off balance because of emotional issues that have buried themselves deep within your body's organs, soft tissues and bony fragments. Detect these vibrational problems before they manifest into complicated issues such as heart disease and cancer, before they are too late to treat by vibrational methods. Once vibrational illness has manifested, you can learn how to reset your cell frequencies by use of forgiveness techniques and other vibrational remedies. Prevent illness from manifesting don't wait until you have to treat the sickness.

Each emotion is stored in a specific location in your body.

For example, issues of love and hate are stored in the heart and its surrounding vessels and arteries. Those who have underlying issues of love and hate will manifest heart disease and arteriosclerosis.

The behaviors and habits of personality are planted in childhood but grow more prevalent with age. Since love is the soul's only food source, issues of love and hate manifest quickly within the body. That is why heart disease is so prevalent.

Many have childhood issues that have never been addressed. They think that because they are grown and no longer have direct contact with the person with whom they had issues, the original problem is no longer a source of pain. However, what they don't realize is that the pattern of behavior remains within them. They treat the people with whom they share their lives as though these people are the cause of the pain. Therefore, the cycle of love and hate continues. The heart, in trying to eliminate these feelings, constantly produces antigens that ultimately manifest as heart disease. This cycle can be stopped by forgiveness of that original sin committed upon the child.

The body is an amazing machine; it forgets nothing without the mind requesting it. When requested by the mind and with adequate effort, the cells can be retrained to vibrate at a different rate, thus changing the course of illness. You are in complete control of your body; your body is not in control of you. With knowledge of the working systems of your body, you can change the course of disease and illness.

The body has many neurotransmitters, neuropeptides, enzymes, proteins and acids that must all work in conjunction with one another. When even one of these is too high or too low, your body recognizes the difference and responds accordingly. Proteins begin binding to other materials in an effort to repair the cellular levels within the body. The body attempts to maintain these levels consistently, so when you take in unhealthy substances and emotions, your body has to constantly work to repair the levels, thus manifesting disease and illness. The body is a machine and requires certain fuel substances to make it work properly. You would not put oil into the gas tank of a car and expect it to work properly. So why would you expect to put unhealthy substances into your body and expect it to work properly? These substances can be tangible substances, such as food, or intangible substances, such as negative energy and negative emotions.

What do you mean by negative energy?

Negative energy is intangible substances, such as gamma rays and electromagnetic transmissions. Many individuals don't take seriously that these types of substances are very harmful to the body. Gamma rays literally destroy the cell-making ability of the body. Electromagnetic transmissions can cause the body to manufacture weak and defective cells, resulting in tumors and other abnormal cell growth issues. You need to understand the importance of what you put into your body and the importance of proper maintenance if you want to live a healthy life while on this planet.

When one has lack of emotional support in his life, he will likely manifest back, hip and leg issues related to the tendons, nerves, ligaments and muscles.

If someone has vertebrae disc or joint problems of the legs and hip, you will probably find they worry excessively about financial issues.

If a person has issues with the fingers or hand, you will likely see they are having trouble holding on to things they value the most, such as time, home and family. The severity of the difficulty in the body will be indicated by the number of fingers or hands involved. The more fingers or hands involved, the more severe the problem. These areas will ultimately have difficulty because of arthritis, carpal tunnel syndrome, neuralgias, myalgias and other tendon or ligament issues.

Having issues with arms and shoulders means one needs to evaluate relationships with a spouse, children and those one values the most. This indicates that the balance of events in ones life that relates to one's spouse, children and those one values the most are out of sync with the demands in physical reality, such as work, are at issue.

Sleep problems cause many things to function improperly. Sleep deprivation is a problem many have but don't realize they have. They need to understand the requirements of sleep for their own bodies. As to their clarity of mind, they will get forgetful and cloudy, which, of course, has its consequences. No need to elaborate on all of those, because they are many.

Kidney problems can mean one spends too much time "filtering" on one particular emotion without taking action. The kidneys are one of the body's filtering organs so when one is over-filtering, one's kidneys can get overworked. By getting overworked, the kidneys tend to develop stones, peritonitis, hypertension and kidney infections. Blood disorders that relate to improper kidney functioning can also manifest.

Those who have problems with bladder control, holding urine uncomfortably, the ureter, bladder infections, kidney stones and other related problems need to examine emotions that have to do with lack of control. They may also have problems that relate to their thyroid and hepatics.

Lung problems indicate that the lungs are having difficulty filtering the air they breathe. This kind of problem can have a variety of causes, including the pollution that is so bad on the earth. Typically it is related to emotions associated with affection, or lack thereof, such as in a relationship with a spouse. When people feel they are not as valuable as the air they breathe, then they wonder why they should breathe in the very thing that sustains them.

The lungs are another of the body's filtering systems. The lungs can become overworked and clogged, causing allergies. Allergies cause the sinuses to be backed up. Stop "filtering" all the things you need to do and just do them. Organize your life so that there is time for all the things you need to do and stop thinking that you are always "going to do them."

Thyroid issues revolve around handling the mechanics of daily life and setting healthy boundaries. The thyroid is the regulator of the body's systems relating to too much and too little. If the thyroid is ill, there will be too many or too few enzymes produced; each condition has its own set of problems. In addition, the thyroid regulates heat in the body and heat can have problems all its own. Too much heat can cause dysfunction in the heart, lung, kidney or liver, to name just a few of the problems.

The thymus is another regulator of the body that is associated with lack of energy and lack of love for life itself and can manifest in those who have a lack of will to live.

When someone has liver problems, it is because of issues relating to the inability to absorb the information about the problems in life. Liver problems always have something to do with not accepting what is fact. This causes the liver to become hard and unable to function, not to mention the damage caused by substances one might use when trying to forget what is fact. Refusing to accept what is in life causes the liver to produce excess proteins and enzymes in order to cleanse

Pancreatic problems imply trouble getting the grit out of life. The pancreas regulates the amount of acid released to digest your food. If you produce too much, you will get ulcers. If you produce too little, you can become constipated and bile will backup in your intestines, which can cause cancer of the colon and intestines. Problems of the pancreas are associated with not being able to keep the clutter out of your life as it relates to the things that make you squeamish, such as a mother-in-law or a needling boss. If a person has too much bitching in their life, the pancreas produces too much acid in an attempt to remove the bitching.

Bile duct problems indicate problems eliminating the toxic waste from life that may come from those people who constantly dump their problems on you. Whether they come to you for your time, your sympathy or your money, it doesn't matter–they dump. For example, if your brother comes to you with a list of bills and a sob story, he is trying to dump on you in order to take the load off himself. If you fall for the story and give him the money but resent doing so, your bile duct will try to rid the body of the resentment by producing enzymes to secrete bile. If there is no bile to secrete in the intestines, the bile enzymes cause the intestines to digest themselves, so to speak. The bile duct can also back up and cause problems in the stomach, pancreas or esophagus if not cleansed properly.

Gallbladder problems show that a person needs help removing stress from his life from repeated dumping. Because of this dumping, the biliary system has accumulated too much bile for the body to handle. The large intestine literally starts hardening to keep the dumping out. For example, if a disabled mother allows her 30-year-old son to live with her without paying rent while she lives off of food stamps, she is allowing him to continually dump on her. Another example would be the big business man whose secretary takes advantage of him by continually calling in sick, having baby-sitter problems or asking for advances. She leaves the dump for him to clean up. He won't fire her, though, because she is the sister of his son's wife.

Colon and intestinal problems indicate the inability to deal with life's kinks, such as your child wrecking your new car or your going to the store twenty times because you are so distracted you keep forgetting what you went to the store to get. These kinds of things cause the intestines to draw up in knots to keep the kinks out. The intestines get too dry because the kidneys and adrenals are responding to the stress and subsequently the intestines cramp.

The pituitary balances everything. Thus, pituitary problems indicate issues of balance, such as having too many demands on one's life–children, home, job, spouse, civic work, etc. In an attempt to limit the demands on one's life, the pituitary starts shutting down.

Ever notice the heightened sense of awareness or tenseness you feel inside when you think of something that makes you upset or when the police officer turns on his blue light behind you? That sense of awareness or tenseness triggers the body to go into defense mode in order to eliminate the sense of heightened awareness or tenseness. The anxiety produced by thinking about the problems causes your body to undergo changes in an effort to stop the painful emotion. Hormones, amino acids and antigens are just a few of the substances released into the body. This unnecessary release has consequences. It can cause your body to deteriorate at an accelerated rate. Forgiveness and acceptance changes these things. When you can think about an issue and no longer experience that tenseness or heightened sense of awareness in your body, you know you have released it.

You have to understand that the person with whom you are having conflict is doing the best he can. He is also trudging through life and learning life lessons, many of which are with you. He is learning as a direct result of the consequences of your relationship together. He is also facilitating for you the life lesson(s) you requested to experience. In actuality, he would be doing you a disservice if he did not do the things he does. You would have no opportunity to learn the lessons you are learning, and without them, how would you ascend?

CHAPTER 29

Life Lessons and Ascension

Most people think they cannot be happy because of this or that, but everyone can be happy if they choose to be. People can find happiness in anything if they try to connect to God. Even those in starvation can find happiness in their lives. Think of the starving people in Africa who are happy at the mere song of a bird in the tree. It takes their mind from where they are and makes them happy. Happiness is a choice of free will and available to all. Even people who suffer depression can find happiness if they put forth effort. Through the power of your own mind, you are able to be happy. Happiness is not unobtainable and is meant for everyone, not only a few.

What about people who are depressed, sick or poverty stricken? How could they possibly be happy?

You wonder why depression, poverty, sickness and all of the other maladies even exist. They are all life lessons, chosen by the individual so that lessons can be learned. Life lessons are only as hard as you yourself chose them to be. They are not placed upon you by God or anyone else, for that matter. They were chosen by you before you incarnated into this life. We are all here to grow, and without the pressures of life lessons, how would we grow?

Life lessons will only help you ascend to where you are trying to go. It is your own goal to experience life lessons. Life lessons are what you are here for; without them, you would have no reason to be here. The lessons enhance your soul, not the other way around. Life lessons will strengthen your soul in preparation for oneness with God.

To be one with the ultimate Oneness, one must know all that the ultimate Oneness knows. To reach this goal, one must learn and be educated with spiritual knowledge. This knowledge can be obtained by intently listening to the silent knowing contained within you or by learning life lessons.

For example, poverty is a tool one can use to learn gratefulness, dignity and appreciation. It is certainly not a punishment, but an experience for growth and learning. It teaches the ability to receive gratefully and with dignity. Poverty is an advanced spiritual lesson and should be admired and respected. It should be looked upon with your eyes as great and not as an oppressing, embarrassing and lowly experience. It takes great ability to endure and it is something that all have to experience.

Sickness is also an advanced lesson and hard to endure as well. It teaches lessons of endurance and empathy. It also teaches compassion and patience. Sickness allows you to depend on others to take care of you and to experience the lesson of shame. Such as the shame of someone else having to clean your feces, feed you and dress you.

Suppression, also known as oppression, teaches a tangible knowledge of love for freedom of life without control and; a knowledge of love without control. Suppression is not an easy lesson to endure and should also be admired. Souls who choose suppression are strong souls who endure much. They should be applauded and recognized as examples of growth, for they learn much about life.

Life would not be worth living without the lessons you learn, especially the hard ones. Be grateful for the lessons and learn them with dignity.

Happiness is meant for all and is a choice of free will. It is you who allow the negative thoughts to remain within you. Choose not to house them. Think of the things that do make you happy. Put forth the effort to move towards those things and happiness will find you. It took time for the unhappiness to take hold and it will take time for it to leave, but leave it will if you choose to remove it from your thoughts.

CHAPTER 30

Ascension of the Soul

Soul lessons are learned by individual souls throughout life incarnations and are all lessons of value. They are necessary for a soul to advance to the Oneness. For a soul to advance, it must learn all of the life lessons the akashic records identify. The akashic records are the records of a soul's existence. Once these lessons are learned, the soul will be allowed to keep ascending to the light of God. (We choose to use the word God because that is what Eva understands. We had to use terms she would understand in order to dictate the book. You may use any form for your descriptive understanding of the ultimate Oneness of all there is. It is all the same. The ultimate energy is the ultimate energy, no matter what it is called.)

All souls are required to learn their lessons before ascending. Souls are also required to go through seven levels of ascension. These seven levels of ascension are required for a soul to actually face and become one with God, the ultimate energy. God is omnipresent and has to prepare souls to be in God's presence.

What is meant by omnipresence is that God is all-knowing to all souls, all there is to everything, all-knowing to all things, all that can be to anything, all things could ever want to be, all things that are, and all things will be. Souls cannot just ascend directly to God because they would be incinerated. A soul is pure energy and would not be able to stand the omnipresent energy of God without the preparation obtained through ascension.

Souls are allowed as many lifetimes as they need to prepare and learn the required life lessons; it is all determined by free will. Souls will always be required to ascend to God before facing God. God will always be omnipresent, and souls will always have free will and ascend. They will also be required to learn about God and God's way of being omnipresent and everything that is or ever will be. All souls are eventually to be one with God through ascension and learning. All souls and God are one and the same. All souls are pieces of God and eventually will be one with God through ascension. And through ascension, all souls will eventually be omnipresent and one with God and all souls will eventually be all there is, as is God, and omnipresent.

CHAPTER 31

Parallel Dimensions and Levels of Ascension

A soul has but one purpose in the physical reality and that is to ascend. The purpose of ascension is to be one with God–"God" being the ultimate energy, and the ultimate energy being all there is in a universe of many. Our universe is but one universe in a system of many universes. In order to actually face and become one with God, souls are required to go through levels of ascension, one of which is the level of physical reality as we know it. The purpose of experiencing a dimension is to obtain the knowledge to ascend. If you don't learn what you are supposed to learn at each level, you have to repeat the level until you do learn the lesson.

Well, how many levels or dimensions are there?

There are eleven dimensions in all, but only seven are attached to ascension–meaning that there are seven dimensions in which you would experience in order to ascend to the oneness of God. It's as if there are eleven "classes" you can go to, but only in seven of those classes do you receive a report card. The other four classes are elective classes where you can go to be healed and prepare yourself for the next level. These elective classes are necessary to the soul because after each level of incarnation, the soul contains negativity (electrons) which needs to be removed before continuing. This is because after each level of ascension, the soul will contain residual negativity that has to be removed.

(1) Reality as you know it is but one plane of existence and consists of earth and all that is three-dimensional.

(2) The next plane beyond the physical would be what you consider to be the plane wherein discarnate souls reside before they are able to ascend. There is no ascension attached to this level. This level is not much different from the earthly plane except that you don't inhabit a body. All your thoughts and emotions continue to exist. At this level, there are no physical boundaries and there is no physical body. Here the soul has to move to the light and has to know that it can go to the light, or else it remains stuck. If souls think they are in hell, they will stay at this level and experience what they think of as hell. All they have to do is change their thoughts and say, "I am in the light, "and they will be in the light._

(3) The next plane is the causal plane of existence. It is an advanced plane, also known as the teaching plane. It consists of what you would understand to be the level of wisdom and higher learning of spiritual awareness. It is where the guides of mankind reside. Only souls who have spent time on at least two levels of the seven levels attached to ascension are able to inhabit this plane for wisdom of humanity is essential.

All souls on this plane have for some reason decided not to incarnate in order to spend time teaching those who are on the earthly plane. Both Michael and I reside on this level for the time being. It is not a punishment; it is our desire to teach that brings us here. For without teachers, learning would be much harder to accomplish. We can continue our path of ascension at a time of our choosing.

(4) The next level is the level of recovery from the physical plane. This level is for cleansing souls of negativity that they took on during the physical lifetime. This is not a level of ascension, but a level for healing purposes only.

(5) The next level, the level of intelligence and integrity, is attached to ascension. You would understand this level as mass consciousness. Although this level is experienced in physical form utilizing a body, here it is experienced with much greater intellectual capabilities. The beings on this level are more evolved than human beings. They communicate entirely by telepathy and do not have the food requirements of human beings. There sole source of food is energy in the form of electromagnetism. The reality of this dimension is also different in that it is multi-dimensional, meaning it has more than six dimensions. Souls who reside here have completed at least three of the seven levels attached to ascension.

(6) The next level, also attached to ascension, is the level of loss and deprivation. A soul spends time alone learning and feeling the experience of a void universe and experiencing the total lack of love. This reality is not a physical reality but one of pure energy. A soul cannot exist without love and therefore the learning process is short. It takes about two years of time as

you know it. A soul cannot bear much more than this without withering and dying, having to start the process all over. Because a soul's sole source of food is love, it cannot do without love for much longer than this. This is the hardest type of love to experience in that a soul has to find love for itself in a universe void of all it recognizes and associates with love.

Again, I'm not sure I can comprehend what you are trying to get across.

In other words, the soul is all that will reside in the void universe and must learn to love itself without direction. The soul has to depend on itself to teach itself to love.

Does the soul even have knowledge of its objective purpose in this dimension?

The soul has the knowledge that its objective is self-love. It has only to find love in a state of complete aloneness. The soul has to ultimately realize that it is all there is and that it contains the ability to manifest love in any form it needs. Once it realizes this, the soul can manifest a complete world if it desires to do so.

That is the nature of a void universe–to fill the universe with love as the soul defines that love. You can compare this to what God originally experienced in the beginning except this love is experienced by the single soul.

Is this existence experienced in a physical reality?

It is not experienced as a physical reality, but through thought processes alone, much as a dream.

(7) The next level you would understand to be the level of the progression of will. This level, also a level of ascension,

is not a physical reality but a level of thought and outcome. A soul must think of a scenario and experience its outcome as if it were actually experiencing it. This takes place in the fashion of simulation within the confines of the soul's existence. This simply means that the soul will experience alone, without the consequences involving others.

The level of the progression of will is designed to establish a great growth of knowledge for the soul's repertoire of experiences of love and emotion. Without this knowledge, a soul would not understand the oneness of God and all there is. This level is hard to endure because there is no one involved in the scenario with whom to share your shortcomings. This growth mechanism is too painful for many to bear, and many souls give up and decide to become guides at this point.

The level of the progression of will helps souls fully understand the power of free will. Free will is not all there is, but rather what it is not.

What do you mean "what it is not"?

In this dimension, the soul lacks the luxury of free will and has to learn to develop free will over a period of repeated experiences.

What do you mean "develop free will over a period of repeated experiences"? I don't understand.

Well, for example, a soul will be told it has to do a certain thing and the soul wants to do that certain thing because it was told to do so.

I suddenly had a picture of a computer doing a given task that we program it to do.

Yes, Eva, much like a computer. The soul must ultimately figure out that the things it is being told to do are not always in its best interest. It has to learn to love itself enough to develop the will to object to those things it does not feel are in its best interests.

How are these things experienced? Are they experienced in physical form?

These things are all experienced in a form somewhat like simulation.

Somewhat like the simulator of the Chevy Show at Six Flags where you feel like you are driving an airplane or racing over a mountain in a car? Or perhaps playing a simulation game on a computer?

Yes, computers are a form of simulation. The soul does not actually inhabit a computer but uses such a device to effectuate the experience. It will all make sense as your understanding of the multiple dimensions grows. The experiences gained through the simulation process are all felt by the soul as if the experiences were its own.

(8) Because the previous level leaves a soul emotionally dead, so to speak, the next level is another level of healing. It is not attached to ascension.

(9) Next is the level of learning to face God and become one with everything, also a level of ascension. A soul must learn to combine what it is with everything that is. This is not as easy as it sounds. A soul will resist departing with who it is and must

endure the hardships associated with that.

Is this level experienced in a physical reality such as life on earth?

It is not a physical plane as you know it, but it is a physical plane in a sense. A soul is tied to physical reality as it relates to free will. It behaves as if it is a single unit, though it is not. On this level, the experience is that of a mass consciousness experiencing itself united as one. In order to be one with God, a soul must let go of who it is and be one with all there is. A soul carries an identity throughout its existence and it is hard for the soul to release this identity of itself as a single unit.

(10) At the next level, the level of purification, all negativity is cleansed before the soul ascends to be one with God and all there is. There is no ascension attached to this level, as it is a level purely for spiritual cleansing.

Tell me, how is a soul cleansed of the negativity?

On this particular level, electromagnetism is used to remove all negative particles of energy in the form of electrons that remain in the soul's essence. These particles are particles of electrons that have remained within the soul due to hate and lack of love.

Could we use electromagnetism to remove negativity from our souls while we are on earth?

Yes, electromagnetism could be used on earth to removed negativity. However, it must be used at a certain frequency to accomplish the results sought. The wrong frequency could cause devastating effects on mankind. Dannion Brinkley understands the frequency that we are referring to.

(11) The next level, which is attached to ascension, is the level before uniting with the oneness of God.

This last level is the level of allowing a soul to experience somewhat the feeling of the oneness to help determine if the soul is truly prepared to reunite with the Oneness of the Ultimate Energy of all there is. This level allows a soul to observe from a distance the Ultimate Energy of all there is.

On average, how many lifetimes does it take to get to this level?

A soul who reaches this level has completed approximately 10,000 lifetimes. About one-third of those lifetimes are spent on earth. You must remember that multiple lifetimes are lived simultaneously, so it is actually more than 10,000 lifetimes as you would know it.

How does a soul know for sure if it is ready to be reunited?

It can feel the energy of the Oneness and if its energy properly resonates with the Oneness, it is ready to reunite. If it does not properly resonate, it must figure out what it lacks and return to the appropriate level of learning for the knowledge it needs to reunite.

How will it know if it resonates properly with the Ultimate Energy of all there is?

The soul will know if it is ready or not by the frequency of light it emits from its being. If it is not ready and attempts to reunite, it will be extinguished and have to start the process all over again, for the energy of God is great.

Would being extinguished be a punishment for attempting to reunite without being ready?

It would not be a punishment but a consequence, two distinctly different things. The soul knows beforehand that it must be prepared for reuniting. God doesn't extinguish the soul; the soul extinguishes itself by attempting to join an energy greater than its own, much like trying to burn a piece of wood in the heat it takes to heat a piece of steel. Obviously, the wood would burn up long before the steel even began to get hot.

Okay, that seems perfectly logical. I understand now. How does a soul actually reunite with the Oneness?

Reuniting with the oneness is a three-step process. First, the soul agrees to reunite and lose its identity of self. Next, the soul loses its ethereal body and the knowledge of all that was and accepts the knowledge of all that is. Lastly, it combines itself with the ultimate energy as one.

What do you mean loses the knowledge of what was?

Well, a soul cannot retain its knowledge of its singular experiences. It has to receive the knowledge of all there is.

CHAPTER 32

Descriptions of Existence in the Parallel Dimensions

Lifetimes on earth are probably the easiest of all lifetimes because the remaining lifetimes are geared toward advanced spiritual growth. However, life on earth is also the most emotional experience of all the dimensions because of the physical aspect of touch and sexual intimacy.

You manifest your own physical reality, and love in the physical reality (sex) is probably the most intense love you will experience. The actual experience of lovemaking is the most intense form of love within all dimensions. The act of love can be expressed in many ways, but the act of lovemaking is the most intense. The act of lovemaking without love attached is not what we mean; that is merely a sexual act. The act of expressing true love to a mate is what we mean. The act of expressing true love to a mate is love uncompared. True love is a most intense emotion. It is unparalleled in all dimensions and a sight to behold in the eyes of both mankind and God.

Let's take Romeo and Juliet, for example. They loved beyond all physical means. They loved beyond all else. They loved with true intent to be together until the end of time. This is the kind of love of which we speak. Love of this nature exceeds all limits of physical reality. Love to this extent is love like no other.

CHAPTER 33

Love in the Multiple Dimensions and Mass Consciousness

Love in the multi-dimensional realities (meaning greater than six dimensions) is love experienced by all simultaneously. It is like the love you experience with your children. It is more of a compassionate, caring love than an intense emotion. It is more like feeding spiritual nutrition to the life of the soul. The soul in multiple dimensions simply needs love to exist and love is the only source of food needed by a soul.

Does the soul inhabit a physical body within these dimensions?

The soul in multiple dimensions does not inhabit a physical body such as the bodies inhabited on earth. It lives in more of a mind-over-matter state, manifesting what it needs when it needs it. There is really no need for a physical body, though experiences can be experienced through a physical body if need be.

I'm not sure what you mean by this.

Well, imagine a soul living in a colony of thought. When it needed to experience something, the entire colony of thought would experience the experience. For example, if you needed to experience the taste of eggs, the entire colony would experience

138

the taste of eggs. You would, of course, have a reason for the need to experience the taste of eggs. You would take that reason to the Council of Thought to have the experienced approved. Once approved, the Council would manifest the taste of eggs. That way it would be experienced by all with consensus.

Are you allowed to have separate thoughts or must every thought be a thought of consensus?

Separate thoughts do exist. They are just not manifested without consensus.

Other dimensions are far less emotional. Lifetimes on the other physical planes are more involved with the mass consciousness and lessons are learned differently. Life in other dimensions is experienced more as an understanding rather than an emotional involvement. On earth, there is more play and less seriousness and lessons are learned on an individual as opposed to mass basis. Though mass consciousness does exist and is utilized on earth. In lifetimes involving mass consciousness, lessons are experienced and learned collectively.

In mass consciousness, the elements of emotional pain are the same as they are for you on earth, but there is more wisdom available. Because the emotional pain is experienced by all, it is different than having to experience the pain alone. The emotional pain experienced in mass consciousness is more of a compassion and sorrow type of pain; you either knew or should have known that a particular behavior would result in a particular consequence. But because the initial problem was misdiagnosed, the entire consciousness would suffer. The lessons are also tolerated as one, so the results are experienced simultaneously by all. The entire population contributes knowledge and the decisions are made by consensus.

The after mass of the world trade center bombing is a classic example of mass grieving.

With so much collective knowledge to contribute to the decision-making process in mass consciousness, how would mistakes be made?

Mistakes are made by misinterpreting the actual problem. These lessons are more about the moral lessons of people's needs. The lessons are for the benefit of all. Life without these lessons would be fruitless for the soul. A soul hungers for knowledge like a baby hungers for its mother's bosom. Knowledge helps the soul ascend to the oneness of God and that is its whole purpose.

Can you describe the type of consequences a mass consciousness would experience?

It would be very much as if the people of the earth had one government without an appeal process so that any decision made by the governing body would affect the entire population.

Is mass consciousness experienced in a physical body?

Yes, mass consciousness is actually experienced in a physical body of some sort. We know you have problems grasping this concept. The extraterrestrials that have been seen are actually souls who are experiencing mass consciousness. Souls experiencing mass consciousness are souls who understand the concept of manifestation. They have learned to manifest themselves into other dimensions in order to learn and grow.

Well, you are indeed right. I do have a problem with the concept of extra terrestrials and UFOs. I've always thought they really didn't exist, and I have to admit that I still wonder.

You can't change what is to suit your belief structure.

I hear you and I'm trying to understand.

CHAPTER 34

An Understanding of Your Universe

The universe as you know it, is not what it seems. It is a universe of one, in many. It is one universe with many solar systems in a universe of one in many. Because your universe was created by the masses of all the solar systems at one time, it is created and experienced by the masses simultaneously; all dimensions are experienced at once. That is why there is a horizontal energy field. This energy field is caused by the space between the dimensions where all excess negative energy is stored before being recycled back into the universe.

All dimensions contain negative energy remnants from thoughts and motive ill used. Since energy never stops it has to go somewhere so that is the somewhere. That somewhere is contained within the womb of God and is available to all for a manner which is appropriate. The energy is clean energy so to speak. It has great potential for mankind. It has the potential to move consciousness and mankind into the next millennium and save the earth at the same time. It can solve the rainforest issues, the water issues, the ocean issues. It can provide everything that is needed by the entire universe at one time.

You are not alone in the universe and the energy sought

must be sought with respect for all. If not, the others utilizing the energy will become hostile and another problem will start. If the energy is taken in the form of liquid gases, then all hell will break out. It must be taken in the form of hydrogen molecules and then changed into what you need. Hydrogen molecules are large enough so they can be captured and then changed into the form needed. They must be captured when the sun is on the far side on the location needing to capture them. They must be captured by a mechanism to keep them from cooling more than 20 degrees centigrade. If they cool more than that then the energy will be lost and wasted into a non-usable energy form.

Another form of energy and the most viable source of course, is the sun. The only problem is that the economics of the sun doesn't work for the greedy. The greedy need to understand that new technology for its use would require jobs to manufacture the technology. All the world would win.

There is also stellar energy. This is the energy released by stars and planets when they breath so to speak. This is different from the energy recycled from God's womb. This is energy that was compressed over time and is released by the breathing of the solar systems. A solar system inhales approximately every 600 days. That is why there are solar flares which are more distinct about every 600 days. The way to capture this energy is by magnetic engines. These engines will operate on nothing more than magnetic energy which is caused by the flux of the solar systems. The magnetic engines will run off magnetic opposition which would not be possible without the energy flux and the magnetic poles to absorb them. That's why it is available to all, because it is everywhere.

CHAPTER 35

A Discussion of Multiple Dimensions

There have been many books written on levels, dimensions and parallel universes. How do we know which theory to believe?

Aside to the Reader: I personally had a problem with publishing a book announcing there were eleven parallel dimensions. I knew and still know nothing about parallel dimensions. Why someone would believe me I had no clue. So, a few nights after the harmonic concordance when I initially received the information on multiple dimensions, I had insomnia and was flipping TV stations. I stopped on the discovery channel, which was on a commercial at the time, put the clicker down and got up to go to the bathroom. When I came back, the show on that night was "The Elegant Universe" and they were interviewing Edward Witten and he was explaining the M Theory of the Unified String Theory. I sat in disbelief because there being described on television was the physics formula for what I had just channeled.

The Unified String Theory supports the existence of eleven parallel universes. Physics is a science that reflects the law of what is, as it relates to reality. It is the law of what is, and the law of what will be. Physics is not only about computing numbers to assess equations but also about manifesting your reality as it relates to all there is and, of course, all there will be in the parallel universes. Physics is simply the application of imagination, free will and intent, limited only by your imagination and your limits to be.

Physics is always provable by computation, so how can you deny the existence of what is proven. If one has a computation available setting forth what we have told you, how can one deny what we have said? By the mere computation of a math problem, you can piece together the facts of what we have said, for physics has no objective except to reflect what is. It has no ego to inflate and no personality to boost in the eyes of man. It simply is what it is.

Okay, Eva, let's discuss multiple dimensions. We know you personally have some doubts about the issue of experiencing multiple dimensions simultaneously, but, as you know, ultimately the facts will be what they will be. And the fact is, souls do indeed experience multiple dimensions simultaneously.

I cannot understand how we can experience things simultaneously and not realize it.

If we could only explain this in a manner you could understand. Let's see…souls are able to experience on multiple levels of consciousness just as you have several dreams occurring at the same time. Think about the phonograph record your father told you about. Imagine each song on the record as a lifetime, and all the songs (lifetimes) are playing at the same time. But because they each require a needle to play, the needle representing the frequency of the dimension being played, you can listen to only one at a time. If you had eleven needles, you could play the songs of all the dimensions at one time. However, the body in physical reality as you know it, can hear the song of only one dimension at a time. But in REM (*rapid eye movement*) sleep, you can catch a glimpse of dimensions other than what you are living. You can glimpse all of the dimensions, if you desire to do so, but only in REM sleep unless you raise your frequency to that calibrated for each dimension. REM sleep provides insight to the soul as to all dimensions, for you have multiple simultaneous dreams every night. It is this insight that we are trying to bring to your attention for it is this knowledge that benefits the existence of your life as experienced today in physical reality as you know it. With the benefit of this knowledge, your soul's growth experience is greatly enhanced. For with this knowledge, you enable yourself to avoid much pain typically experienced with soul growth. Because you will possess a greater knowledge base from which to draw from, you will make wiser, more intelligent decisions that will ultimately alleviate negative karma that one typically incurs by making poor choices associated with soul growth. We cannot explain it any better than this.

I didn't realize we have multiple dreams all at the same time.

Although you think the multiple dreams you are having at night are occurring one after the other, they are not. You simply remember only those occurring during the period of your sleep you know as rapid eye movement (REM) sleep. You may have ten dreams per night but only remember the various parts of dreams that occurred in REM sleep.

Why do we only remember the dreams in REM sleep?

This is because REM sleep was designed so that the psyche could look into the soul if it chooses to do so. All of the information of all of your experiences is there within the soul. But not everyone is ready for all of the information at once, so it is given in the form of REM sleep.

Well, how do we access it?

Now, when a soul is ready to view all of the information, it is available in the same way you receive all other intuitive information.

Well, that's not logical to me—to not realize that you are experiencing things other than what you realize.

Of course it is logical. The body has limitations and overloading it is one of them. The reason you yourself aren't aware of the other things you are experiencing simultaneously is because you have significant problems with too much input as it is. How many times have you told your children to stop screaming and turn the TV off? God only knows what would happen if you were aware of all the things going on at the same time in the other realities. You would go over the edge. But for those ready to know, the information is there.

Thanks a lot for that comment. Just what I wanted to hear!

Well, we are just telling you how it is so you can relate and understand what we are trying to get across.

CHAPTER 36

Free Will–How God Became

Can you tell me how God became?

Well, in the beginning there was void. The void or the will of God, began to tire of the voidness, so it began to think of becoming something, of what it did not know. It began to develop what you might think of as dust. This was much smaller than dust as you know it, but it was dust just the same. The particles migrated towards one another and formed the beginning of all there is. An accumulation of energy began to grow within the universe due to particles of heat combining with particles of cold. The combining of the two caused an exorbitant amount of energy to be produced. Once the energy was produced, it became charged with positively and negatively charged electromagnetism. The positive and negative electromagnetic particles began to pull together. As the particles multiplied, the mass became larger and as it grew, it began to take on form. Once the particles became large enough for what you would refer to as an ethereal body, the ethereal body began to take on consciousness by the will of the particles to become one over a period of about two billion years as you know it.

How did the particles become conscious?

The will of the consciousness grew over time, much as a baby grows. Just as a baby's mind develops, so did the consciousness of God. If you only understood free will completely, Eva, you would understand all there is. As the will developed, so did the desire to be one with consciousness. As the will of oneness developed, so did the consciousness of God. As the consciousness developed, so did the need for stimulation. God needed intellectual stimulation. He began to manifest his thoughts. He began to visualize what he thought, and what he visualized appeared. That is why you need to understand the power of free will. Free will is the foundation of all there is.

What do you mean by "free will is the foundation of all there is"?

Well, free will is desire and intent, which places energy in motion. When energy is placed into motion, it can change forms. When changing forms, it develops into the object of the original desire and intent. This is the beginning of all there is, taking over six billion years at this point in time as you know it.

Free will originated with the void becoming tired of the voidness. It began to pull energy from within itself to manifest the particles of dust. It did this by finding deep within itself some form of energy, which began the manifestation of the particles. Free will is the underlying foundation of all there is.

Well, where did the energy come from if the universe was void?

The energy came from the desire to manifest, which, of course, placed energy into motion. We cannot explain this any better.

CHAPTER 37

Learning to Hear the Voice of God
Raise the Vibrational Frequency of Your Soul

On another note, why would a soul even want to experience physical reality?

The world of physical reality exists for lessons of heart and mind. The soul learns lessons of the relationship between God and mankind. How mankind is to receive their communications from God must be learned here. Without this information, a soul will never hear God through its own senses. The ability to hear God through one's own senses is vital for ascension. A soul has certain requirements for ascension and that is one of them. The will of mankind makes it difficult to accept that this ability resides within, and that will is what must be overcome within the lifetime. The voice of the oneness of God is always there; it is the will that hides it.

The voice of the ultimate energy can always be heard as long as the soul wants to hear it. The soul is a natural receiver for the information if it is tuned to the right frequency. A soul has a choice of whether or not it desires to receive the information. It all depends on whether or not a soul chooses to vibrate at the appropriate frequency.

How does a soul become aware of and change its vibrational frequency while in a human body?

This is done by allowing the self to accept that all things are a part of the ultimate energy and that the soul is simply expressing a form of free will by incarnating into a physical body. The soul is always permitted to hear the voice of the ultimate energy. It is just a matter of free will. Open yourself to the light of the one energy and you open yourself to all there is. Open yourself to the Oneness of God and you open yourself to all there is.

Can every person "hear" the inner wisdom or just psychics, mediums and the like?

Many people think that the gift is reserved for a select few, but the gift of hearing is available to all. The person must simply accept that he or she has the capability, and the knowledge will come. The soul's vibrational frequency depends on how much awareness it has of the ultimate energy. Its level of awareness corresponds to its vibrational frequency. The vibration of a Buddhist monk will obviously be higher than that of an angry rebel.

What are you opinions on spiritual teachers and gurus?

Spiritual teachers and gurus are wonderful ways to learn the things to do to accomplish your aspirations. However, a spiritual teacher can talk to you all day long for the rest of your life and if you fail to listen you have wasted your time. If the teacher is of integrity you should be able to place your spiritual life in their hands for they will teach you Oneness. If it is Oneness you seek, do what they tell you to do, you will know within you if it is right. Spend time meditating, spend time getting in touch with who you are. The teachers can guide you down this path; but if you fail to listen to the wisdom of All There Is, then the teacher can teach you nothing.

Most people think that a soul is a soul, but all souls are different. Each soul grows at its own rate. No one or no thing can affect the vibrational frequency of a soul unless the soul chooses to listen. Choosing to listen to the knowledge of all there is, does not usually occur because "hearing" is a direct result of increased frequency, not the other way around. A soul vibrates at a lower frequency on the physical plane than on any other plane. The energy molecules must vibrate more slowly so that the density of physical reality can manifest. Think about it, an atom is made up of a nucleus, election and proton which consists of about five percent mass. If everything is made up of atoms and one atom is only five percent mass then all atoms are five percent mass. Doesn't that mean that everything as we know it is only five percent mass? We manifest our reality much like a hologram.

There must be a level of denseness in order for the plane of three dimension to set its boundaries. The earth's population as a whole has an expectation of what they consider the boundaries of three dimension to be. Therefore, the boundaries are limited to the extent of the mass consciousness of the population as a whole. There exists only what the mass consciousness imagines exists. The greater the extent of the mass consciousness, the greater the boundaries of physical reality.

CHAPTER 38

The Reaches of Physical Reality

How far does physical reality reach?

Reality is what you imagine it to be. The soul must allow itself to exist beyond physical reality to fully understand its capabilities within physical reality. That is the entire purpose of the existence of physical reality for the soul to experience manifestation. What is the purpose of living in flesh if the soul is forgotten and the experience useless? The lifetime will have to be repeated and the pain of the lessons not learned will have to be repeated and experienced in greater detail. Life is not about experiencing all the fun you can have without consequences. It is about ascension of the soul. No matter whether one believes it or not, it is what it is and you will all awake to that knowledge at some point. Whether it is now or later depends on the nature of your own free will. It is determined by whether or not you choose to raise your vibration to hear sooner rather than later. Whether you take the road of least resistance and learn the hard way or you take the road of most resistance, which will result in growth and eventual contentment, is up to you. The road of least resistance is the road upon which your life currently travels. For your vibrational frequency to raise, change will be required in your life. It is these changes that we are most resistant to. Change is frightening. Change is the unknown. But once the change is made, we realize it is the path we should have taken all along. It is the path of our longing, we just didn't realize it.

The rate of ascension and growth is based entirely upon your ability to accept manifestation and the knowledge that comes with it. The knowledge of manifestation is a powerful tool for growth, but it is also a powerful tool for destruction. So awareness of consequences is essential.

CHAPTER 39

Where the Soul Goes After Death

What exactly happens when a person dies?

Life after death varies greatly based upon the individual. It will be different for each person based upon their expectations. Typically there will be a period of time for souls to cross over and go to the light. After that they will face a life review committee. They are allowed to take some time in between lifetimes if they choose, but typically this life review is done first.

After a soul spends time with the committee to ascertain the effects of its life on all others involved, it will feel all the feelings experienced by all whose life it touched. The soul needs to understand the effects and consequences of all its behaviors. It is a painful experience to endure and lasts about two hours of human time. The life review experience runs through quickly, though painfully. After that, a soul can go to a place of its choosing based upon what it feels it needs.

Where might a soul choose to go and what do you mean by based upon what it feels it needs"?

These are some of the places a soul might choose to go:

The lightwork wellness center heals souls from harsh lifetimes they may have endured by exposing them to brilliant rays of energy and colors, which heals the chakras. This process takes about six weeks.

Some souls wish to go to the akashic records room to review their complete life history. The soul spends a lot of time here reviewing, learning and studying the lessons learned throughout its existence. It has much material to access regarding its existence and lessons learned. The akashic records room is a focal point because souls continue to utilize these records throughout eternity.

CHAPTER 40

Cleansing the Soul of Negative Energy

Another place souls might go is to the essence of God, which we've discussed before. God's essence is another healing mechanism available to souls who experienced great pain in their incarnation.

They also might choose to go to the heavenly choir of angels to listen to beautiful music and for peace and quiet. Music is always very healing to the soul.

One might choose to go to the yolk of heaven for serenity and peace. There are flowers, fields, grass, trees, lakes, waterfalls, mountains, snow and beauty everywhere. In this place of divine peace, the temperature is perfect for each soul.

The hall of wisdom is the place of eternal knowledge where one can learn about the oneness of God and how God became.

Tell me more about the hall of wisdom. What is it like?

The hall of wisdom is in the essence of God and is hard to describe. It consists of the knowledge of God contained in electromagnetic fields. One would simply go into the electromagnetic field and take in the information.

The room of well being is a place where souls go to heal themselves with water and healing stones. Water with all sorts of stones made of different substances, such as quartz, hematite, sodalite and other stones and crystals are used to heal the soul. This is very healing to the soul because a soul is energy and the energy vibration of the stones and water sets the soul's energy vibration back to normal.

Another place a soul might go is the death room. This is a place where all negative energy is put to death by healing light and water. A soul would elect to use the death room if it had experienced so much negativity that it couldn't be cleansed any other way.

Why would souls choose this room last?

They don't elect this healing mechanism first because it is quite painful to endure and the process takes a rather long time to complete.

Why is it so painful?

Souls don't like to be stimulated by any negativity and here they have to be stimulated with electromagnetic charges of negative energy to pull out the negativity that remains within them.

Why do they have to use negative energy to pull out the negative energy?

Because negativity attracts negativity.

Aside to the reader: Originally, I could not understand this because I always thought that particles that are alike, such as magnets, repel each other. However, one day I was at the bookstore and ran across the book entitled The Body Electric by Robert O. Becker, M.D. and Gary Selden. It was another synchronistic event.

I had no idea why I pulled into that bookstore that day. I was on a tight schedule and there was nothing I wanted or needed. I walked in the door and walked straight to that book. I picked it up and opened it to read the following paragraphs:

"Besides the amount of charge being moved, a current has another characteristic important for our narrative–its electromotive force...

"In high school most of us learned that a current flows only when a source of electrons (negatively charged material) is connected to a material having fewer free electrons (positively charged in relation to the source) by a conductor, through which the electrons can flow. This is what happens when you connect the negative terminal of a battery to its positive pole with a wire or a radio's innards: You've completed a circuit between negative and positive. If there's no conductor, and hence no circuit, there's only a hypothetical charge flow, or electric potential, between the two areas. The force of this latent current is also measured in volts by temporarily completing the circuit with a recording device, as I did in my experiment.

"The potential can continue to build until a violent burst of current equalizes the charges; this is what happens when lightning strikes. Smaller potentials may remain stable. However, in this case, they must be continuously fed by a direct current flowing from positive to negative, the opposite of the normal direction. In this part of a circuit, electrons actually flow from where they're scarce to where they're more abundant....

An electric field forms around any electric charge. This means that any other charged object will be attracted (if the polarities are opposite) or repelled (if they're the same for a certain distance around the first object. The field is the region of space in which an electrical charge can be detected, and it's measured in volts per unit of area." (pages 80-81).

Now everything made perfect sense. I understood how negativity could pull negativity, leaving only the positive energy remaining.

What happens to the energy once it is pulled out?

Once the negative energy is pulled out, it is recycled and placed back into the universe.

How is it recycled?

It is recycled by being placed back into God's womb.

CHAPTER 41

Learning Processes of the Soul

Another place where souls can go is the hall of affirmation. This is where a soul goes to learn if the life lessons learned actually taught the lessons set out to learn. The soul meets with its council of nine and reviews the lessons set out to learn compared against the lessons actually learned during the incarnation. If the lesson was learned, the soul gets to put that lesson behind and move on to another. If the lesson was not learned, the soul will have to relearn the lesson either through reincarnating or through another soul's lessons, the latter of which is preferable, if possible. A soul may learn lessons through observing other souls during its incarnation but the lesson must be learned from all perspectives before it is considered learned.

How is this determined?

The committee assigned to the hall of affirmation decides if the soul learned the lesson or not.

What if the soul disputes them and says that it was learned and they said it was not?

If the soul disputes the committee's decision, it can appeal to God for a hearing. This is a rare occurrence, though, because the committee consists of very wise and old souls who are fair and impartial.

Next is the room of denial, where a soul goes to learn lessons of denial and refusal to give love when needed. The soul does not elect to go to this room. It is mandatory to experience, much as a mandatory college class. It is a rather painful experience and not one a soul looks forward to attending. However, a soul understands the necessity of this room and attends without remorse and with glad heart.

The room of whither and wonder is where a soul can learn to be a guide if it so chooses. Lessons are taught about consequences, cause and effect and how to instruct others on the physical plane while the soul is in the causal plane, or teaching plane. This room is for souls who do not wish to reincarnate again within the near future.

What is considered the near future?

Somewhere between two hundred and three hundred years.

Another choice would be the hall of respite, where souls learn to deal with anger they experienced due to lessons they had to endure while incarnated. It is a painful room to endure since the soul will have to watch his own behavior played out for all to see and will experience the indignation that its behavior caused in others. In this way, the soul finds out what actions were actually appropriate. Then the soul will experience the effects of its appropriate behavior had it chosen to act appropriately.

There is also the hall of exaltation and ecstasy. Here a soul can feel the ecstasy and exaltation of the omnipresence of God.

Can you describe what happens here?

It is hard to explain, but it is similar to a sexual orgasm except that it is experienced by simply being in the presence of God.

But I thought you said that if a soul was before God without being ready, it would be incinerated.

A soul can experience God's presence without facing him. Facing God and experiencing God are two completely different things. A soul can experience the light of God's presence. When a soul faces God it literally faces God, eye to eye, so to speak before being allowed to ascend to the next level of ascension. What transpires is a total all encompassed, tantric (which literally means "woven together"), resonating (coming from the Latin word "resonare" which means to vibrate. A process of knowing between two beings, the one that knows and the one that wants to know, in order to experience harmonious emanation and radiance of the two) expression of love between God and the soul. Such is similar to the feeling of a sexual orgasm but much for vitalizing for the soul and its being of who it is, with everything that is.

Is the light of God's presence the same as the light of God experienced when a soul crosses over?

The light of God's presence is more intense than simply the light of God. It is the light extending from God's actual presence, not just the light extended into heaven. The light of God is the illumination of heaven. We hope that makes sense. It is hard to describe in a way that you can understand.

EVA HERR   AGAPE–THE INTENT OF THE SOUL

CHAPTER 42

Why Some Souls Don't Cross Over

Can people really communicate with their loved ones after they pass over?

If a soul has important issues that remain after it returns to God, it is allowed to return and deal with the issues. That is why some people see a loved one after he or she dies, as you saw your father. Some souls have a hard time letting go of loved ones and have to go back and revisit them to resolve certain issues.

Are there reasons why a soul would not cross over?

For various reasons, some souls have a hard time crossing over. For example, their frequency gets off, they simply may not be ready to leave a loved one, or for karmic reasons they remain stuck in the astral plane until the issue is resolved. If the frequency of a soul is vibrating at a level that is bound to three dimensional laws, then it will not be able to cross over to the light. The reason for this is that each level has vibrational frequencies that are acceptable ranges in which to blend. If the soul's vibrational frequency is less than the acceptable range for the next dimensional frequency, then it will not be able to blend with that dimension.

Other reason a soul may not cross over is that it loves

the three dimension and the astral plane, or it is not ready to deal with the life lesson review or the negative karma and the accompanying pain of its life review. After a soul has returned to the light of God, only then can it return to the three dimensional plane to address issues if needed. This does not mean that a soul cannot communicate with a loved one immediately after death; it means that a soul cannot deal with the complex issues associated with loved ones until it has been healed of the negativity that remained attached to it when it crossed over to the light of God. A soul can indeed communicate with loved ones while on the astral level. If they choose, souls can remain in the astral level until they are ready for their life review. This is not punishment but a choice. Some souls like to stay on the astral plane for a while. It is enjoyable for them to watch, communicate with and comfort their loved ones. They can stay there as long as they like. However, they do not ascend before God while on the astral level. Since ascension is the whole purpose of a soul, it doesn't remain in the astral plane for any great length of time.

CHAPTER 43

Assistance from Loved Ones Crossed Over

Once a soul crosses, what happens?

Once a soul passes through the astral level, it can begin ascension and move into the light of God for warmth and love if it chooses. Souls are really thinkers and like to think about the lessons they learned and dialogue with other souls and with God so they can grow and learn. They may go with an old soul to discuss their lessons in more depth or they may decide to view their akashic records with their peer group. What they do is their choice. However, their ultimate purpose remains to grow through ascension towards the oneness of God. Sometimes souls will request information from a loved one's akashic records and then attempt to help that loved one accomplish his or her life lessons. Souls are known for attempting to help other incarnated souls with their life lessons.

Souls are required to ascend and incarnate, and they need to learn lessons to do that. You need to be clear on that. Please know that without incarnating, souls have no way to ascend, and without ascension a soul cannot be one with God. Please also know that souls incarnate at their own rate and as long as there is incarnation, there is ascension. Souls who elect not to incarnate will not ultimately become one with God. But after completing enough lifetimes to have gained sufficient knowledge, they can act as guides and can elect to continue incarnating at any time.

Again, souls can only go through ascension if they incarnate. Through incarnation, souls learn lessons and advance through lifetimes. Souls may go through thousands of lifetimes if they choose, incarnating as many times as they like. Souls do not stop being; they are infinite, as is God.

Do all souls have the same characteristics?

Each soul is unique and will not have the same characteristics as any other soul. Souls are as unique as snowflakes, if you know what we mean.

Souls are the interior light of the body and need to shine in order to function properly. All souls are constantly trying to stimulate agape, the internal flame of their light in order to ascend and grow.

What do you mean by "internal flame of their light"?

An example of igniting the light would be for a soul to agree to assist another soul in karmic payback. Karmic payback is not attached to ascension, but it does sometimes kickstart a person into paying attention to its soul. A good example of this would be if a soul while in pure spiritual form, begged for the lesson of misery. Then in order for the soul to learn the lesson of misery, someone would have to inflict misery. No soul in its right senses would want to inflict misery upon another for a soul in pure spiritual form experiences agape for all. Therefore it would be necessary for the assisting soul to inflict misery upon the soul seeking to learn misery. The assisting soul will usually wait until the last minute before inflicting the misery to make sure that the soul is not going to find the right path to learn the lesson before causing the infliction of monumental pain. Inflicting pain is a hard thing to do for a soul in pure spiritual form. All decision for kick starting a soul by inflicting pain is made on the causal plane during REM sleep.

Souls are to God, what people are to souls, in that people have to learn lessons on earth and souls have to learn lessons in heaven. Souls incarnate into bodies to learn lessons for ascension. Souls begin their life review with the lessons they learned during their incarnation. Upon completion of their life review, they meet with their council of nine to apply the lessons learned during the last incarnation to the lessons learned through their existence. The lessons are combined in the akashic records so that they may be reviewed in entirety for the quality of the lessons learned during the existence of the soul. In essence, people learn lessons on earth so their souls can take them back to heaven and learn the details of the lessons. Heaven is where all souls go to continue learning and growing.

CHAPTER 44

What and Where Is Heaven?

Specifically, where is heaven in all that you have described?

Heaven is in the essence of God and is available to all souls at all times. A soul has the ability to access heaven at its choosing. Souls are always allowed access to heaven whether discarnate or incarnate. They can enter heaven at any time. It is all a matter of choice. Souls are not only allowed access to heaven but they are also allowed to bring other souls to heaven in order to teach them.

How would a soul teach other souls in the afterlife?

If a soul takes a loved one to heaven, it will do so through dreams and astral travel. That is why loved ones sometimes experience dreams of the afterlife. Souls are very loyal beings and try hard to be there for loved ones. They try every way possible to assist those members of their soul group who are incarnated on earth. Your father taught you through REM sleep, Eva and that is a good example of what we are talking about. They are constantly trying to teach loved ones about the oneness of God, the ultimate energy. They are always trying to help incarnated souls grow and learn so that they can ascend before God and be one with God.

Souls are what make people who they are. Souls are what make the body alive. Souls are the essence of the body, just as God is the essence of souls. Souls are the essence of life, and life is the soul of creation and eternity. Souls are the backbone of creation, with God being the creation of souls, of course.

Does everything have a soul or just people?

Souls are the single item of existence in the universe. Every living thing in the universe has a soul. Souls are the essence of the universe. Without them there would be no reason for the universe to exist.

CHAPTER 45

Without Peace, the World Cannot Exist

People must be responsible for both their thoughts and actions, for both produce results. There must be peace in the world or the world will be no more. Without peace, love cannot exist and there must be love for the universe to survive. Peace and love are necessary for survival. If there is not peace, God will allow the natural consequences to occur to restore peace. This will not be what everyone is hoping for. The natural consequence of lack of peace is hatred, war and destruction. There will be terrible times for those who remain, with famine, drought, death and despair. There will be no love and no happiness until God restores life to the planet for His return. Only then will there be joy and not before.

Despair will overtake the world if people don't do something now. They need to start treating every person on earth just as they want to be treated or it will be too late to save the world before you know it.

There is not a lot of time to accomplish the things that need to be accomplished. Time is limited. The oneness of all there is, the ultimate energy, is growing weary of the lack of love, of the fighting and hatred. The natural consequences of destruction will occur if something is not done to deter it.

But I thought that everything that occurred was cause and effect and that God did not punish.

What we mean is: all there is, is growing weary of the lack of love, fighting and hatred. If all there is tires, then all there is ceases. Everything in the universe of the earth depends on the survival of the world. The world is one of the magnets for all things within your universe to stay together; without it, the things in your universe will fall apart.

Are you saying the universe revolves around the earth?

Other life systems within your universe cannot exist without the world and they should not have to end their lives because of some who will not evolve. Great karma will be accrued by those who refuse to evolve into more loving beings.

Well, I just hope the scientists don't give me a hard time about this.

The scientists won't agree. They can't even agree with each other and typically they don't believe in God. However, it doesn't matter, because it is what it is. What they think won't change what is.

Time is of the essence and people need to do something quickly before it is too late. If you don't know what to do, simply treat everyone, and every living thing, as you want to be treated and things will happen from there. That will be a big first step.

Tell people to spend more time praying to God for peace so the archangels will work on that. The archangels will work on whatever is asked of them. So if you want peace, you need to get busy with every approach you can think of because negativity is building fast. The more negativity that builds, the shorter the time to correct it so time is of the essence. Spend more time praying for love and it will come. Life as it is now is threatened and people need to understand this. Please let the people know so that they can decide what to do. Life is almost at the point of destruction and people must make some choices before it is too late. Life is a fragile thing and must be treated as such.

CHAPTER 46

Love and The Energy Dynamics of the Soul. Protons, Food for the Soul

Souls are only as strong as the love they receive. More love must be shared in the world or the world will cease to exist, for love is the fundamental basis of all that is. Love is basically all that matters because you can't take your possessions with you. Love consists of protons which are the food for the soul. Without the food that sustains it, it cannot exist and thrive. If a soul does not thrive, it wants. It cannot remember the memory of love and therefore does not know for that which it wants. When a soul wants but does not know what it wants, negativity breeds because it desperate search to fill the desire of want.

Why? Is it like having enough yeast to make the bread rise? Many would say love is eternal.

Because the energy of the world must remain at a ratio that is greater positive than negative to sustain itself. If the energy ratio slips to that of greater negativity, then the world will cease to exist as you know it.

Eternal love has nothing to do with the ratios of positive and negative energy on earth.

Souls are the essence of the universe and love is the single thing that bonds them. Love is the only thing needed for a soul to survive. A soul is the only living thing on earth that has no food requirements except love. Without love, the soul cannot flourish. It will wither and die and grow hard and angry. With love, it will grow strong, flourish like a flower and love in return. Souls are always going to need love and everything continuing in the universe is going to depend on love. Love is the foundation for all that exists. Without love, the universe will cease to exist.

Love is not tangible. It is fed to the soul as electromagnetic energy. A soul's nutritional requirements consist of positive electromagnetic energy. Such energy is released by a soul when expressing love and absorbed by the receiving soul as love. Such an exchange is executed by electromagnetic energy. Love can only be transmitted by positive electromagnetic energy. That is why it is so important for the people of the world to understand positive energy.

Positive energy is the sustainer of life. It sustains the very essence of life as you know it. When you think positive thoughts, you generate positive energy, which is then transmitted through the electromagnetic field surrounding your body. When this occurs, the positive energy negates any negative energy it comes into contact with, thus balancing the scales of energy to a positive force. As more positive energy is transmitted, more negative energy is negated. People need to understand the power of positive thinking, because positive thinking is positive power transmitted to the world.

Love is positive energy (protons) that bond together to

form an electromagnetic band that runs from the source to the receiver.

God's energy consists of all there is but is balanced to a proportion that is greater positive than negative energy. Negative energy is required in three dimension in order to define the boundaries of your existence. It is will and intent that decides if that energy is put to use or not. If the negative energy is never put to use, then it doesn't matter if it is there or not. Negative energy can only be used with negative intent by the possessor of the energy. Negative energy slows the vibrational frequency of the soul, thus inhibiting ascension for the individual soul.

So, a soul lives on a physical substance, protons? I can't help but think you may be using "protons" metaphorically or to substitute for another term that we would not easily understand. [To the reader: the following response was given humorously, as if they were laughing:]

It is positive energy by whatever name you choose to call it.

If a soul is not hungry for love, it has too much negativity to notice that it is hungry. When a soul gets in such bad shape, it only knows that it wants, but it does not know what it wants. It only knows to take everything it can get. To want and not know what it is you want is a dangerous place to be in. For when you are in this place, you take everything you can see in an effort to stop the want. Love has become so unfamiliar to the soul that the soul forgets that love is what it seeks.

The exchange of energy stimulates the electromagnetic field of the receiver, causing the receiver's field of energy to literally change vibrational frequency by slowing the pulse and breathing rate. This allows the transmitter will be able to transmit the energy. If the receiver is not able to receive the energy, it means he is not hungry for food at this time. If he is not hungry for food, it means that negative energy is predominant in his energy field and this negativity is preventing the soul from accepting the positive energy. If a soul is consumed with negative energy, the only way to free it for consumption of protons is to allow it to experience the pain it is causing others.

One can only hope that the soul comes across a source of positive energy strong enough to affect the ratio of protons and electrons so there is more positive than negative energy available in the soul's life; meaning that the family of the soul, assuming it is a loving and nurturing family, can influence the soul's behavior when in contact with the soul. Such a change is hard to accomplish because a soul filled with negativity cannot handle stimulation by positive energy without some life-changing event that will ultimately bring about forgiveness. Such a thing is hard to do without the soul having love for some person or living thing. Without that, the soul has difficulty finding the strength to seek forgiveness for what it has done.

It is much like the kid in the ghetto who steals and robs. He sees no reason to change, for no one cares whether he changes or not. He says, "what is the use?" Until he actually feels the vibrational frequency of "love" and remembers that it is "love" he seeks. Only after he feels the exchange of love will he remember that this is what he was seeking all along. All along he had been confusing "acceptance" with "love" and hadn't realized it. Acceptance was simply the nearest thing to love he could find, so that became the standard. He was accepted by his gang members, but there was no love, no nurturing, no exchange of protons, so the soul was merely residing within the body instead of thriving. It takes the dignity of only one person to change this soul's path, but one person there was not.

The dynamics of energy works something like this. All electromagnetic energy is made up of protons (positively charged particles), electrons (negatively charged particles) and neutrons (zero charge or neutral particles). If a soul is emitting positive energy, it is emitting more protons than electrons. If a soul thinks negative or hurtful thoughts, it emits electrons, or negatively charged particles. Just because you cannot see the energy does not mean it is not there. Electricity is in the wall circuit even though you don't see it. In fact, the energy transmitted by your thoughts is much more powerful than the electricity in the wall circuit, for energy changes forms. Energy changes form much like water changes from liquid to ice. You can feel the water when it changes to ice, but you cannot feel your thoughts turn to violence. It just happens.

Negative thoughts are the sole source of violence. That is how it works. Energy changes forms, ultimately manifesting violence. If negative energy becomes more prevalent than positive energy, violence becomes prevalent, thus the beginning of the end. It is not God who will end the world as you know it. Negative energy will. There will be no quality of life. There will be famine, war and great death—not because of God but because negative energy will be prevalent throughout the world. Like a bomb, negative energy will cause destruction. It is a chain reaction. Negativity breeds negativity. Violence breeds more violence. Through these things will the world become a miserable place, not because of some self-imposed sentence by God, but because of the consequences of negative energy. Because we are all one, any sentenced imposed, would be upon and by one's self.

CHAPTER 47

Oprah Winfrey is But One Person

You have said before that one single soul can change the world. How can one single soul make such a difference as to change the entire world?

This is our response. Oprah Winfrey is but one person, but Oprah Winfrey changed the world. She made a conscious decision to change the world and to change the vibrational frequency of the masses. By making a conscious effort, she set an example for the masses to follow. She evolved in front of them and they evolved with her. She is an example for the minorities. She is an example for women. Because she made a conscious choice to make a difference, she did make a difference. She is an example of what one person can do. Anyone can make a difference if one chooses to do so, each in his own way. It matters not if your way affects the masses or one person; it matters only that you do it.

Oprah Winfrey changed the vibrational frequency of the world, and by doing so she gave hope and faith to many that the soul is indeed infinite. One person can do many things, the significance of which is not always known to that one person; but significant it is. Through the efforts of Oprah Winfrey, violence was kept at a level that inhibited the vibrational frequency of the world from lowering ever so slightly. Thus, the positive energy of the world resonated with the masses, increasing the vibrational frequency of the world and thereby giving people in the world additional time to think of more ways to continue the cycle of positive energy. The level of positive energy created by this one woman, manifested through desire and intent, changed the world for many thousands of souls.

Thank you, Oprah Winfrey, for your efforts. They have not gone unnoticed, for the karma you have created for yourself will be a joy to experience. You may have no idea of the significance of your efforts, but the world is a better place because of them.

CHAPTER 48

The Importance of Teaching Children Love

We would also like to remind you that the children must be taught that love is the single most important issue in the world. All that is, whatever is to happen in your world, has to come with the children making a difference in the world. Children need to be taught that love is all they need to be happy. Love is all-encompassing to a soul and can make great things happen. All people need is love and they can conquer anything. Nothing more is needed to live a happy life, for love is the foundation of all there is. Children need to know these things.

The majority of the children of the world do not know what it is like to feel all-encompassing love. The parents in wealthy countries often express love to their children through the telephone and e-mail. Parents in poor countries love their children by touching them with their arms and hands. Which children do you think feel the most all-encompassed love? Was that a surprise, Eva? You were not expecting that, were you? The average parent in a wealthy nation spends all of their time working and communicate through technology. Many children never get touched. They never get arms placed around them in a loving fashion. There are many, many children like this in the world. We have no idea of what we are depriving our children. But the world is seeing the result in the behaviors throughout the world. Just watch the television and listen to the radio.

Well, I have to admit, that was not what I was expecting.

The majority of the children of the world are growing up stone cold, so to speak, because they are growing up without being touched by the warmth of the fire. Thus, the fire starts waning from lack of embers and eventually dies out, the fire being the parent, of course. Children know only what their parents teach them when it comes to love. Love must start in the home. If it's not started in the home, the children won't learn love, for no one loves children as their parents do.

If the children do not receive love from their parents, how can they love themselves? And if they aren't taught to love themselves, how can they love others? Love for others is necessary for the world to survive. It is imperative to love one another as we want to be loved. Others are just as important as loved ones when it comes to loving behavior.

The people must love every living thing. Respect for God is not what you might think it is. Respect for God is love to all things. It is much more than just loving one another; it is treating all things as you wish to be treated. Loving one another is part of what you need to do, but you must also treat others the way you want to be treated. Most people think that if they love everyone, that is all they need to do, but it is not. You must treat everyone as you wish to be treated.

What is the difference between loving and treating?

In order to love fully, you must behave in a loving manner or it is just a nice idea. Having an idea of love and actually loving are two different things. Thinking about loving all and everyone actually feeling loved is the idea. If the people don't feel the love you are thinking, what is the purpose of thinking the love?

That reminds me of an experience I had the other day. Two friends of my teenager were playing with his ferret, tossing it back and forth and flipping it. They let it drop to the floor, breaking its back. I was mortified and my children were heartbroken. I took the injured ferret to the home of one of the teenagers, whose father was a doctor. We showed up on his front porch, the ferret on a towel convulsing, obviously in pain. My ten-year-old and my four-year-old were standing there sobbing. I said, "This ferret needs to be put to sleep. You are a doctor and your daughter recklessly hurt it. Can you just give it a shot so it will die peacefully?" I was astounded at his response. He told me that it was not his problem. I couldn't believe my ears. Before me stood a healing practitioner who possessed not once ounce of sympathy, much less empathy. I could not believe such profound lack of dignity and integrity.

This man has lacked love all of his life and does not know what it is you feel. Therefore, how could he teach his daughter to love? Medicine is wealth to him. It is not about what he can do for others, but what others can do for him.

Wealth brings with it many things, including notoriety and fame, which destroy most who have it for that very reason—they become obsessed about what others can do for them and not what they can do for others. The souls who choose this life lesson do not have it as easy as one might think. Notoriety and fame are very complicated life lessons because they involve the masses; one is followed by the masses and therefore it requires much responsibility. You must set an example for the people if you choose to live that lifestyle. Fame and notoriety have a tendency to accrue great karmic debt and can have a lot of negativity attached to it when the body dies.

CHAPTER 49

World Hunger and World Peace

World hunger and world peace are very significant problems in today's society and we would like to address these issues. With the accumulated wealth of the world, it is shameful that hunger and starvation even exist. If world hunger is not addressed, world peace will not be obtained. Population growth is out of control in some countries and hunger must be resolved before these countries can work on issues of peace. The people must have adequate food before they can think about the policies of peace and war. Hunger prohibits people from thinking, much less acting. It is our suggestion that the people of the United States and other wealthy countries make it a priority that all have food, regardless of the country's political agenda. The world is owned by all, not just the wealthy. The people of the world are all equal, regardless of their country of birth, and they should all have the right to food and sustenance. Once the food issue is resolved, the people should be provided information about birth control. The world can only hold so many people.

World peace is not going to happen on its own. The people need to make this decision as a mass consciousness. This will only be done with mass attention and specific policies on peace by the governments of the world. Every person should treat every other person as they want to be treated and that should be the doctrine of the world. Each person in the world should love his life, for he is responsible for manifesting its content. The people of the world need to understand that love of life is essential for peace. Without love of life, there can be no peace.

For example, if we could say something to President Bush this very moment, we would say this:

June 29, 2004: If you want to facilitate peace to the beheaders *(talking about the violence in Iraq and in the middle east)*, then continue doing exactly what you are doing… killing everyone in site and taking over the world. However, if you *really* want peace, then you need to understand that these people are people and they are fighting a cause. The problem is neither really understands or considers the other's cause. You need to understand that these people want their old country. They don't want modern society. You need to remember that these people have lived this way for thousands of years and want to continue doing so on a mass consciousness level. Whether you admit it or not, mass consciousness exists and you have to abide by the laws of the universes that the masses control the country, not an individual. An individual contributes to the masses, but an individual must make a big noise to be heard over the masses. The masses want peace, but they want what they want and that want is to return to their lifestyle. They will grow at their own rate, not that of your choosing. It is your choosing that angers them. If you would repair the old instead of building the new, you could stop the beheading.

Now, they need to understand that it is your goal to help, not hurt. They are of the opinion that you are attempting to overtake their country. Tell them you will redistribute some funds to rebuild the old and let them grow at their own pace and you will see a big difference in their behavior soon. They need to know your intentions are good and they will stop their aggressions.

You will know we are telling the truth because the last marine taken shall not be beheaded.

We are just trying to help, we are wise beings with many lifetimes under our belt and if you listen, you will find favor with the world. The only reason one would not listen would be for personal gain and we know that you are of more integrity than that. So we applaud you in advance for your work to save the world.

Please remember that Eva is just our messenger, respect her as you would respect yourself because these are not opinions belonging to her. She has no opinion in this regard.

And that is what we would say to President Bush.

To the reader: If you recall this was when the Lebanese marine was taken. He, for whatever reason, what return unharmed around the first week or so of July, 2004.

CHAPTER 50

Love of Life for What It Is

What do you mean by love of life?

People need to understand that the life they are living is the life they themselves chose and that the life they are living is the life they need to live in order to learn the lessons they have chosen. Without the life they are living, they would not learn the lessons they chose to learn. Without the lessons they chose to learn, they will not ascend. Without ascension, they will not be one with God and that is the whole purpose of a soul.

Life is meant to be loved for what it is. If you cannot love your life for what it is, how can you expect anyone else to love the life they are living with you? Life is like a home movie. It needs to be edited and lived in the best interests of all participating and it needs to be shared with all who are important to you. Without sharing, there is no purpose to life. Love is the foundation for all there is. A soul needs to be loved, and love is gained through sharing. Through sharing and receiving love for one another, we feed the masses.

CHAPTER 51

Money, Prosperity and Wealth

What are your thoughts on "money"?

Money is the root of all evil.

But you said that money on its own is not a terrible thing.

What we mean is, the attention given to money is the root of all evil. The currency itself is not evil, but the importance placed upon it. People love it and it makes life not worth living. It has great power on earth and people kill for it. Money has great control and causes people to hate. People need to put money into the proper perspective as it relates to God and humanity. They forget that life is much more important and should be put first. Money is the single largest cause of violence. Money should be used for necessities and not to compete. Money on its own is not a terrible thing. It is the emotional attachment to it that is so terrible. It should be used with discretion. People should be aware of their personal motive and intent for using money.

Love is directly related to prosperity and giving, as prosperity is a direct result of loving life as it relates to one's own life lessons. When one loves life and prospers, one needs to give to those less fortunate so that all can enjoy the bounties of the earth. If one shares the prosperity, one will be rewarded with more prosperity in the future to come and the prosperity will not cease to exist. Giving a portion of one's prosperity is an expected requirement of life and should not be overlooked. Through giving, we learn to give graciously and without resentment and others learn to receive with dignity. People need to learn that giving and receiving are necessary life lessons to be learned by all and that life is useless without them.

Money is a gift. If it has been bestowed upon you, it should be shared with those less fortunate. It should be shared with gratitude and not with contempt. If money is shared with contempt, the gift of giving is not bestowed upon the giver. The giver actually incurs negative karma because he releases negative thoughts when giving the gift. Negative thoughts place in action negative energy, thus defeating the whole purpose of the initial giving.

When you choose a lifetime containing wealth, one of the lessons that goes along with the wealth is learning to depart with wealth. You must learn to part with wealth graciously and not with power, greed and vengefulness. If you use wealth to seek vengeance, you will be sought with a vengeance in your next lifetime. This is the law of cause and effect. In other words, what goes around comes around.

If your wealth is used to corrupt business, in your next lifetime your business will be corrupted by those seeking to corrupt business. You will spend your lifetime running from corrupt business and the related consequences of the judicial system. In essence, what we mean is use your wealth for the highest good, because what you use it for will be manifested in your next lifetime.

Love is the only mechanism by which money or other charity can be given or received, otherwise negative karma will be incurred. Money and charity must be given and received with love. If it is given or received with contempt, negative energy will be in effect and the giving and receiving efforts will be lost in negative karma. It is not about how much is given but about the quality of what is given and the gratitude with which it is received.

CHAPTER 52

Who Answers Prayer

Love in the world is so much more important than anyone knows or realizes. It is the sole purpose of all that is. (How did you like that play on words?) Love allows people to grow within themselves. It makes for peace and happiness and families and jobs and wealth and abundance and health and laughter and safety from fear and hate. It is all that people need to accomplish the goals they have in life. The people need to strive in everything they do to spread this message across the world.

Well, what if they don't spread it or don't want to spread it?

It is certainly their choice not to do so, but I have heard literally billions of prayers asking for guidance, so here it is in black and white.

When we pray to God is the prayer actually handled by God, by angels or by guides?

God is the ultimate energy of all there is. If he hears a prayer, it is heard by all there is, because we are all one. We, as angels, souls, guides or any other adjective you care to come up with, are simply extensions of the knowledge of all there is. Regardless of which extension responds to a prayer, God is still responding because we are all one and all there is.

Let's take a prayer of hope for the health of a relative. This prayer is heard by all there is; the extension of all there is that responds to prayers of hope for the health of a relative will respond to that prayer. So, you see, God is ultimately responding to all prayers through extensions of himself. Does this make sense? If not, we can explain it this way.

If there is a light that shines upon a neighborhood, the light will be seen by all. If you are inside your home, the light would appear to be only in your home. Unbeknownst to you, that light is being seen by all who drive through your neighborhood, and therefore the light is not your light but their light too. The wisdom of God belongs to all who choose to use it. Therefore, we can all assist with problems as long as we draw from the same light. The response will be the same, just as the light is always the same whether we are inside the home or just driving by the home.

CHAPTER 53

Do You Want to Resolve Conflict? Practice Love

The people have only to pass the knowledge and then practice what they preach and their prayers will be answered.

This seems too simple. How can we know if practicing love is working? For example, how can the Arabs and Israelis utilize this to resolve conflicts, especially when they have different spiritual figures, such as Allah, Mohammed, God and Jesus Christ?

Well, how does it make you feel when you practice this theory of love? Does it make you feel good? Does it make you feel as though you made a difference in the life which you it practiced on? If so, you have answered your own question. If not, it makes us wonder if you really paid attention to the person you practiced upon. If you pay attention, you will notice a change in the body language and pulse of the person upon whom you are practicing. They will exhibit behavior that is relaxed and loose as opposed to stressed and rigid. By these things you will know that the effects of loving behavior are working.

Now, as to the varying spiritual figures, that is the whole purpose of this book. Love is the same, regardless of what figure you choose to follow. You know what they say: *[At this point, I heard the tune to "When You Wish Upon a Star" from the movie Pinnochio.]*

> *When you wish upon a star*
>   *[the star representing the ultimate Oneness]*
> *Makes no difference who you are*
> *For when you wish upon a star*
> *Your dreams come true.*
>
> *When you share love with your world*
> *Makes no difference who you are*
> *For when you share love with your world*
> *The peace will come.*

See, we do hear more than our heavenly choirs; we hear Jiminy Cricket too! [*They had exhibited humor throughout our dialogue and I could hear it again here.*]

Now let's see how serious the people are about their prayers because this knowledge, the knowledge of Agape, is the answer to all their prayers for peace in the world.

If the people do decide to pass on the knowledge of agape and treating others like you want to be treated how long would it take to obtain peace?

How long it takes to obtain peace in the world will be a direct result of the amount of commitment put forth by the people. It is all determined by the free will of the people. It is in their hands.

What will motivate the people to practice and spread love?

The people will see results based on the effort they put forth. We cannot do it for them; that would be interfering with their free will and we do not interfere with free will. So, the people need to know that results are dependent upon the effort put forth.

However, they no longer have the excuse that "I am only one person, I don't know what to do...." For now they have the answer, *Agape.*

CHAPTER 54

The Power of Forgiveness

That was the end of their message. I was awestruck, all I could think of was how grateful I was that I had been given such a wonderful privilege of receiving this information. I thought, thank you so much for such a wonderful task and for coming to know you, Michael, Seth and Thomas.

"We didn't give you anything, Eva, you earned it," they replied.

I thought, what do you mean I earned it? I did nothing.

"You earned it, my dear, when you learned the true meaning of agape. Unconditional love and forgiveness, for your mother. Love and forgiveness is what it's all about, you see. If you can love and forgive, you can heal the ailments of your life! *The day you forgave your mother, is the day you could hear. That was the moment your vibrational frequency raised to the point of hearing clearly.*"

My God, I thought. I had never realized that until this moment. I would never forget the day I actually forgave my mother, so profound was the experience.

I started "hearing" bits and pieces in March of 2003. In May of 2003, I first became aware of Michael when the channeling abruptly started that day in my kitchen, but the communication line was not clear like it is now. I was receiving some interesting information, but certainly not the kind of information contained in the depths of this book. I did not receive the deep information in this book until after my friend Leslie came for a visit.

Leslie had always popped in and out of my life, and in June 2003 she popped in for the first time since the tarot reading the night of the fire. I was excited to see her and began telling her about my new "gifts." We sat down and I began a reading for her. First, the young man who had died in her house came through, telling her that she would know it was him because the wind chimes blew when there was no wind.

Leslie burst into tears, explaining that a few weeks earlier she had bought a wind chime. She had noticed that the chimes would blow when there was no wind. The young man told her that he had felt no pain and that he had been grateful for all she had done for him. He said he was pleased that he was able to help her through his death. Leslie had been recently divorced at the time, had three children, no money and her house needed a lot of maintenance. Since the fire so was destructive, her house was razed and through her homeowner's insurance she received a completely new house with completely new furnishings.

He explained that it had been his time to go, but he had been able to help her by facilitating his death through her home. She had given him a place to live when he had none, and he repaid her by giving her a better place to live. What goes around, comes around.

As Leslie sat there sobbing, all of the sudden my mother

came through. She said, "Please tell Leslie that I am sorry for telling her that you were not a good mother."

Tears welled in my eyes and I looked at Leslie and asked, "Did my mother tell you that I was not a good mother?" Leslie sadly put her head in her hands and nodded affirmatively. I couldn't believe it.

"How dare she!" I said angrily. "How dare my mother haunt and harass me in life and then have the nerve to continue even after she is gone." "I just did as you asked" my mother said to me. "In another lifetime you were my mother and you stole my husband. I had to do what I did. I loved you enough to hurt you so that you could learn the lessons and pay back the karma. Without learning the lessons and paying back the karma, you would not ascend and the whole purpose of the soul is to ascend."

In that very moment I finally understood that what goes around comes around throughout lifetimes. I suddenly saw the whole scenario. While in spiritual form, I had asked my mother's soul to help me learn the lessons and pay back the karma I had incurred by stealing her husband. She had simply been a facilitator of my life lesson and the payback of incurred karma. I understood what had happened and that her actions had been necessary for my growth. Had she refused, she would have done me a disservice. She could have chosen a better way to teach me, but teach me she did. And in that moment, I forgave her completely.

For the first time in many, many years, my soul felt

completely free of the anger I had harbored for so long. I could think about all the things my mother had done and not experience the tenseness in my stomach, that sense of heightened awareness that did not feel good within me. I know now that is what it's all about, *Agape*.

A LETTER FROM SETH
TO THE PEOPLE OF THE WORLD

Re: *Agape, The Intent of the Soul*

To The People of The World

This letter is being dictated by Seth on behalf of the Agape book. This book is meant to raise the vibrational frequency of the masses. It has taken us about ten months to dictate this book and we would like this book presented to the masses as a tool for the brave new world on the horizon. With this book, you can teach yourself to hear the voice of All There Is.

   You can teach yourself to manifest anything you desire. But one must be careful what one desires, for great responsibility comes with manifestation. Manifestation can make or break a life. Responsibility comes with manifestation and all the results thereof. Responsibility for all happiness and all grief that comes with that which you manifest. Responsibility for both yourself, and for any recipients attached to you, for manifestation is a powerful tool. You can teach yourself to become observant of the synchronicities that lead you to your destination by just paying attention to those road signs in life.

   We have brought this book to you at great sacrifice of many people's lives. Many people have had to experience tragic occurrences in their lives just to raise their frequency enough to comprehend the contents of this book. Many people have had to lose their loved ones, their assets and the balance in their lives just to teach you. Many people have given up things important to them, just to help the world and All There Is. Agape, unconditional love and forgiveness, it is this that we teach. For if you ask these people, they will say it was worth every step of the way. The best part though is yet to come. These people can teach you these skills without your having to give up those things important to you. With these skills you can have a happy life. You can have all those things wanted for a life of fulfillment and the only thing required for developing this skill is, Agape.

Now, take this book with love and gratitude for it will change your life if it is your desire to do so... all for simply loving your neighbor as you love yourself.

Remember, Agape is the intent of the soul.

–Seth, Michael and Thomas
By and through Eva Herr, a grateful accomplice

PS: Our thanks to all who have contributed their lives to this work...you know who you are.

Printed in the United States
37707LVS00007B/214-264